A Case For Life
Christian Ethics and Medical Science

By
Dr. Bo Kirkwood
with Drs. Ron and John Kirkwood

© **Truth Publications, Inc. 2018. Second Printing.** All rights reserved. No part of this book may be reproduced in any form without written permission from the publisher. Printed in the United States of America.

ISBN 10: 1-58427-274-0
ISBN 13: 978-1584274-8

First Printing: 2009

Truth Publications, Inc.
CEI Bookstore
220 S. Marion St., Athens, AL 35611
855-492-6657
sales@truthpublications.com
www.truthbooks.com

Table of Contents

Preface...7
Chapter 1:   Introduction—A Historical Perspective 11
Chapter 2:   Embryology—Determining Personhood................24
Chapter 3:   Cloning 34
Chapter 4:   Stem Cell Research................................43
Chapter 5:   Birth Control and Artificial Fertilization...............52
Chapter 6:   Sexual Ambiguity and Chromosomal Abnormalities 64
Chapter 7:   Gene Therapy and Gene Testing......................79
Chapter 8:   End of Life Issues.................................84
Epilogue 92
Glossary 94

Acknowledgements

This book is a collaborative effort and, though chapter 3 was by Dr. Ron Kirkwood and chapter 4 by Dr. John Kirkwood, we all consulted and discussed these topics over the last two years while working together in our family practice office in Pasadena, Texas.

There are many people to thank, as this book would not be possible without the help of those individuals. I personally owe a great deal of gratitude to my lovely wife, Cherry, who spent countless hours assisting me in the preparation of the book as well as contributing her input and drawings. I would also like to thank Dr. Toby Kirkwood, my son, for contributing and sharing some of his ideas and knowledge, particularly regarding Chapter 4. Also my sons Luke and Danny were helpful with their valuable feedback. I especially would like to acknowledge the brethren at Parkview for their input and criticism in preparing this book. Finally, I would like to thank Marianne Ubben for suggesting the title of this book.

Dr. Ron would like to thank his wonderful wife, Cyndi, for all her help as well as his daughters, Leah and Kelsey, for the encouragement and proof reading.

Dr. John thanks his daughter, Kelli, for her help in preparing his chapter. He would also like to thank his beautiful wife, Joy, for her encouragement and support.

Finally I would like to thank Mike Willis for his assistance and the Guardian of Truth for agreeing to publish this work.

All biblical references were taken from the New American Standard Bible.

Bo Kirkwood, D.O.
Pasadena, Texas
April 20, 2009

Facts

1. All diseases except trauma have a genetic component.
2. We all have genetic defects.
3. There is research that purports that there are genes for infidelity and even spirituality.
4. Technology exists today to produce large numbers of embryos for *in vitro* fertilization, to select for the most optimum collection of genetic material.
5. In 2000 "optimal" college women throughout America were solicited for their eggs to the tune of $80,000 per donation.
6. There are now more than 25 different ways to create a baby.

To know the mighty works of God, to comprehend His wisdom and majesty and power, to appreciate in degree the wonderful working of His laws, surely all this must be a pleasing and acceptable mode of worship to the Most High, to whom ignorance could not be more grateful than knowledge.

Copernicus

It is not good to have zeal without knowledge, nor to be hasty and miss the way.

Proverbs 19:2

Dedication

Dedicated in Loving Memory to:

John Arvel

and

Lillie Mae "Tootsie" Kirkwood

Preface

And Jehovah God formed man of the dust of the ground, and breathed into his nostrils the breath of life; and man became a living soul (Genesis 2:7).

The gift of life is a precious blessing God has granted each and every one of us. The fact that we exist is a veritable miracle unto itself. The average male produces billions of sperm in his lifetime and the average female produces hundreds of thousands of eggs in her lifetime, of which only a fraction ovulate. Not only that, but only one-third of fertilized eggs ever fully develop into a viable individual. The likelihood of any unique person being born is infinitesimal. Nonetheless, we are here and each one of us is a unique tapestry.

For most of history, mankind knew very little about disease, the biologic processes of life, and the mechanisms of reproduction. Since the discovery of the microscope by Leeuwenhoek in the seventeenth century, biology and knowledge in the medical sciences has progressed exponentially. Man's incessant quest for immortality has produced incredible changes in medical science and, in the last century, we have made quantum leaps in our treatment of diseases. Things that once belonged in the realm of science fiction are now commonplace. Treatments for diseases and surgical procedures that were impossible just decades ago are now taking place in community hospitals. Organ transplants, joint replacements, bone marrow transplants, plastic surgery, and robotic surgeries are now being done on a daily basis throughout the world. We can even change a person's sexual anatomy through surgical procedures!

Not only that, but medical science has now made diseases that once were feared and incurable, exceedingly treatable and life is being extended and prolonged as a result. We now have drugs for almost everything. There are new antibiotics to treat infections. Cancer is no longer the automatic death sentence it used to be with well over 50% of cancers curable with current chemotherapy, surgery, and radiation treatments. We have drugs that effectively lower blood pressure, lower cholesterol, lower blood sugar; drugs to go to sleep, drugs to wake us up, drugs to make us happy, and drugs to increase our attention span. We even have drugs for better sex, which a plethora of television advertisement attests to. And the list goes on and on.

The future promises to have cures for even more diseases. Recently, under the direction of Dr. Francis Collins, the Human Genome Project has mapped out the DNA of man. This, along with advances and other discoveries in genetics and nanotechnology, and the advent of bacterial engineering, along with stem cell research and gene therapy, give hope for treatments and even possible cures for such diseases as muscular dystrophy, Parkinsonism, spinal cord injuries, heart disease, multiple sclerosis, burn injuries, and many, many more. In fact, gene therapy, although in its infancy, may be the key in curing more than 4,000 genetic diseases affecting 1 in 10 of us, including disorders such as cystic fibrosis, Alzheimer's disease, Huntington's disease, hemophilia, and colon cancer. One futurist has even predicted by the year 2030, the life expectancy of man will be 130 years!

Medical science has also made tremendous discoveries and advances in reproduction biology. No longer is pregnancy just the result of physical union of man and woman, but now "conception" can occur *in vivo*, that is artificial insemination, and even in a "test tube" by *in vitro* fertilization. The first "test tube" baby, Louise Brown, born in Great Britain in 1978, was indeed unique, but now in vitro fertilization is common representing 1% of all pregnancies. Reproduction can also occur through cloning and mankind may very well be on the verge of cloning the first human being. Scottish scientists at the Roslin Institute in 1996 cloned the first mammal, "Dolly," a sheep and most recently, a scientist, Dr. Samuel Wood, out of La Jolla, California, cloned cells from his own skin, producing several cellular divisions.

Not only has medical science changed methods of reproduction, new technologies have also changed the method of preventing life. The invention of the birth control pill in the 1960's was indeed a paradigm change. We now have multiple options for birth control, including barrier methods, tubaligation, and sadly abortion. Since the Supreme Court legalized abortion in 1973 in *Roe v. Wade,* abortion has seemingly become the birth control method of choice for many women. In fact, 4 in 10 pregnancies are estimated to end in abortion and approximately 1 in 3 American women will undergo an abortion at least once in her life, with an average of over a million abortions occurring per year in the United States in the last two decades.

Yet, with these medical and biological advances come serious ethical and moral questions. For example, does man have the right to "play" with life? Are certain experiments using human tissue, such as stem cell research, in violation of God's commandments? Is cloning ethical and would it ever be morally right to clone a human being? Does a person have the right to surgically change his or her anatomy to "become another sex"? Can a Christian be involved with *in vitro* or *in vivo* fertilization? What happens to the estimated 200,000 fertilized eggs currently stored in over 360 "in vitro clinics" throughout the United States? What happens to donated sperm and ovum in these processes? Has the Human Genome Project opened a Pandora's box? How will gene testing in the future affect our decisions regarding treatment and what are the potential misuses of genetic information? Does genetic engineering run the risk of becoming a promotion of "eugenics" bringing into remembrance the abuses in Nazi Germany? Are we born with certain predetermined tendencies that cause alcoholism, drug addiction, gender ambiguity, and homosexuality? And would it be right to "choose" the genetic makeup of our future generations?

The question then is where does one turn to answer these serious moral, ethical, and spiritual issues. Certainly, we cannot rely on human philosophy to make such decisions. Unfortunately, humanistic thoughts pervade secular society and are contributing to the moral crisis that exists today. God is no longer publicly recognized as setting such norms. Nor can we rely on human government to answer these questions. Legalizing abortion certainly does not make it right in the sight of God. The government's attitude toward the dignity of life can also be seen in the Terry Schiavo case of 2005. Governor Mike Rounds of South Dakota, in signing legislation outlawing nearly all abortions in that state in 2006 stated, "In the history of the world, the true test of a civilization is how well people treat the most vulnerable and most helpless in their society." Unfortunately, it would seem our federal government has dropped the ball in this regard.

Christians need to take the lead in these matters. We believe the Bible can and *must* answer these modern day ethical and moral questions posed by medical science. The apostle, Paul, wrote to Timothy in his second epistle, "All scripture is inspired by God and profitable for teaching, for reproof, for correction, for training in righteousness that the man of God may be adequate, equipped for every good work." The Bible is not a book of science nor does it specifically address issues such as stem cell research, *in vitro* fertilization, and cloning. This does not mean, however, that the Bible is completely silent in regards to modern science. Scriptures deal with life, death, the duty of man, man's responsibility to God, and man's responsibility to his fellow man. Christians have enough spiritual ammunition to deal with everything modern science has to throw at us. The sanctity of life belongs to God. Man cannot create life nor should he unjustifiably destroy it. But when precisely does human life begin? In the process of reading this book, you may find the answer is not quite as simple as you think. Certainly, the question of when ensoulment takes place may never be answered by man. Furthermore, when does life end? The simple answer may be when the spirit separates from the body, but once again only God may know the precise time when that occurs. Deuteronomy 29:29 states "The secret things belong to the Lord our God" and these questions may fall into that realm. Through the inspiration of Holy Spirit, Paul said, "Each one of us will give an account of himself to God" (Romans 14:12). It is our hope through the understanding of the Holy Scriptures as applied to the current and future scientific advances, each individual can render a righteous judgment concerning these matters.

The purpose of this book is to help the individual answer these serious questions medical science has left us with, though in some cases we may ask more than we can answer! We will come to certain conclusions, some of which will be the opinions of the authors, understanding as humans we are fallible though God's Word is not. With no apologies we will use the Bible, which we believe is the inspired Word of God as our guide. It is not in the scope of this book to discuss the evidences (both internal and external) for the inspiration of the Bible, which are myriad. For those so interested we recommend Josh McDowell's excellent book, *The New Evidence That Demands a Verdict*. We will of necessity look at the science behind the most recent medical discoveries. We will begin, however, with a look at pertinent biblical passages and a brief overview of ancient man's beliefs regarding conception and reproduction.

Chapter 1
Introduction – A Historical Perspective

The earth is the Lord's and all it contains, the world and those who dwell in it (Psalms 24:1).

There was a time when you and I did not exist. There was also a time when you and I began to exist. But when? You might say obviously at conception, but what does that mean? It may confer a different meaning to each of us. It is a very important question with powerful ramifications. It is not trivial! Some may argue what difference does it make; it does not affect me personally. "I can be a good Christian without knowing this." While this is true, when personhood begins will affect our attitude towards birth control, abortion, stem cell research, and even emerging genetic therapies.

In one sense our beginning had its origins with Adam and Eve. The entire genetic material inherent in Man's DNA was placed there by God and has been there, passed down to generations since the beginning of Man. The variation seen in all Mankind is contained in chromosomes with some estimated 3 billion base pairs in every cell. We all share 99.9% of the same DNA yet each of us is unique. Yet it serves no practical purpose to say that we all "began with the first Man and Woman." This does not really help us in determining the beginning of personhood.

To help determine personhood, judgments must be

made based upon knowledge. Opinions based on emotion, fears, prejudices, and ignorance of biologic facts are not logically sound. Albert Einstein once said, "Science without religion is lame, religion without science is blind." Deductive reasoning is a requirement and should not be discarded. People are persuaded to become Christians by such reasoning and the apostles such as Peter and Paul used deductive reasoning when convicting the gainsayers and so should we.

At this point it is important to define some basic words. When we talk about the beginning of personhood, we must distinguish between the words "Life," "A Life," and "The Individual." Skin tissue in a pitre dish is human life. This is not to trivialize the matter; we should respect all forms of life. However, when we talk about "a life" we are talking about an "individual person" and not just live human tissue. Sperm, ovum, and even human skin cells, are all human life, but are they individuals? Of course they are not, yet they have potential with the right circumstances to become individual life.

We should also consider the words "conceive" and "conception." We tend to use these words actively when their use should be passive. Pregnancy and conception are not technical terms. Used passively, they confirm the idea of a woman receiving a developing being. Used actively, they are sometimes used to describe fertilization, especially the word "conceive." Anyone who took biology in high school understands at least to some degree how fertilization occurs and most use the words "conceive" and "fertilization" interchangeably when they should not. It is the passive use found in the Bible and we will elaborate on this shortly. Certainly, the idea of the "moment of conception" is a mental construct and confers no real scientific significance. Obviously the word "conceive" does have meaning, but it is not "fertilization." Luke states in Chapter 2 of his Gospel, conception occurs in the womb and this is precisely correct.

"Fertilization" is a modern scientific finding and has only been realized the last 100 years or so. Experiments carried out by German embryologist, Wilhelm Roux in 1888, confirmed his theory that a "fertilized egg receives chromosomes and shares chromosomes from both the male and the female." This sharing of chromosomes then triggers cellular division. About forty years later, Hans Spemann, and his student Hilde Mangold, introduced the concept of an "embryonic organizer"; that is some substance occurring in the developing embryo that causes it to become organized and develop specialized tissue such as bone, muscle, brain, and other cell lines. With this experiment, Spemann and Mangold spawned a new era in embryology. We now know that human embryos eventually develop some 220 different cell types. Just how this process occurs is still unknown.

Before our present knowledge, Aristotle's belief in human reproduction and development prevailed for almost 2,000 years and significantly influenced thought in Western civilization. Three hundred years before Christ, this Greek philosopher and biologist, proposed the traditional understanding of the origins of the individual that prevailed until the middle of the seventeenth century when his views began to decline. Interestingly, of late there has been a resurgence or revival in favor of some of Aristotle's ideas.

We will briefly review Aristostle's paradigm, keeping in mind Aristotle formed his theory, not based on scientific observation, but rather on "common sense" realism, as clearly he did not have before him present technology and knowledge. As a result, there was little objection to his "metaphysical" principles at that time. Aristotle believed the male was the efficient cause of human generation through the *pneuma* of the semen. Through interaction with menstrual blood, a vegetative or nutritive soul is acquired and life begins. The *pneuma* then causes growth and development to occur and when basic organs of sensation arrive, the sensitive soul "arises," this occurring at about the fortieth day of gestation. Later, through some unknown mysterious process and divine intervention, the "rational soul" appears. Now, the developing fetus has the ability to enjoy "vegetative, sensitive, and rational life."

As mentioned earlier, Aristotle's views on human reproduction prevailed for almost 2,000 years, influencing European philosophers and theologians such as Thomas Aquinas. Aquinas agreed with Aristotle that human conception was not complete until the fortieth day after intercourse (except for the female whom conception is not complete until the nintieth day!). Aquinas also believed that completion of conception could only occur after the possession of the "intellective soul." Aquinas further felt the human embryo became a human being with the development of different organs.

Aristotle's views began to fall out of favor by the end of the seventeen century with experiments made by the eminent anatomist William Harvey. His observations of reproduction in deer refuted Aristotle's views. In that same century, Flemish physician, Thomas Feyens, and a Roman physician,

Paolo Zacchias, began promoting the belief of the rational soul and the living organism beginning at "conception." The seventeenth century also heralded the development of the microscope with Ludwig Von Leeuwenhoek, perfecting it in 1678 to a degree that the human spermatozoon could be observed. Niels Stenson one year earlier had concluded that the female ovum was necessary for reproduction. By 1683, Leeuwenhoek suggested life began when the spermatozoon impregnated the female ovum. With this, mankind began an understanding of reproduction that was finally following the right line, though it would still be two centuries before fertilization was observed.

Still, seventeenth century man believed in preformation. Two views prevailed. One was known as animalculism or spermism. In this view, the ovum was there simply to receive and nourish the sperm. It was felt the sperm contained a very small person perfectly preformed. The Homunculus, as it was called, began to grow once it came in contact with a fertile womb environment. The second view, similar to this, was known as ovism. Here, the

The concept of a homunculus (Latin for "little man," plural "homunculi"; the diminutive of homo, "man") is often used to illustrate the functioning of a system. In the scientific sense of an unknowable prime actor, it can be viewed as an entity or agent.

"**Preformationism**," a theory of heredity, claimed either the egg or the sperm (exactly which was a contentious issue) contained a complete preformed individual called a homunculus. Development was therefore a matter of enlarging this into a fully formed being. In the days of **preformationism**, genetic disease was variously interpreted: sometimes as a manifestation of the wrath of God or the mischief of demons and devils; sometimes as evidence of either an excess of or a deficit of the father's "seed"; sometimes as the result of "wicked thoughts" on the part of the mother during pregnancy (wikipedia.org/wiki/homunculus).

ovum contained the whole future organism and the spermatozoon acted as a "spark" to ignite the growth. Obviously, these ideas of preformation, though prevalent through much of the eighteenth century, were finally discarded and put to rest by Roux's experiments of the late eighteen hundreds.

With our present knowledge of genetics and reproduction, we now understand fertilization involves the mixing of chromosomes from the male (spermatozoon) and female (ovum). We understand this does not happen in the womb or at intercourse but hours later, and even then does not occur instantaneously, but over a period of time involving many factors. In the next chapter, we will discuss this in more detail in our quest to determine the beginning of personhood. Before that, we must look at biblical principles and biblical precepts.

The essence of Christian ethics is the spiritual and moral principles put forth by the Holy Spirit in God's word. The antithesis of Christian ethics is violating principles found in God's word. Current biomedical ethicists unfortunately do not adhere to religious or Christian morality. In fact they abhor it speaking with the most unflattering of words towards those espousing a religious ethic. Instead of using God as their standard, modern bioethicists, for the most part, have turned to humanism and philosophy to define ethics. Many are utilitarianist and consequationilist philosophically. Utilitarianism adheres to the idea of "the greatest good for the greatest number" and is a form of consequationilism meaning that the moral worth of an action is determined by its outcome (the ends justify the means). Its origins are credited to Jeremy Bentham, an eighteenth century philosopher with its most well known proponent today being Peter Singer whom we will discuss later.

The acceptance of a utilitarian ethic is unfortunate because it fails to give dignity to the individual life. It also justifies certain medical research based on the common good of humanity rather than accepting the concept of right or wrong. As a result, those who define morality based upon right or wrong are considered "religious bullies" because of their dogmatic views. Interestingly, modern bioethicists are dogmatic in their condemnation of religious dogmatism!

It is important then to understand in our approach in this book, we are adhering to a Christian ethic where right and wrong can be defined and an individual's rights and dignity are considered precious. God is the ultimate standard and His will is revealed by His words. We believe it is very important to decide which ethics you are going to follow. Bioethicists defend their position by saying although they do not follow a religious ethic, they still have *an* ethic. In response to this, where any ethic will do, you have no morality. Adolph Hitler had an ethic!

Bioethics should not and cannot be separated from Christian ethics, which rest on the foundation of the moral and spiritual laws found in God's word and His son, Jesus Christ. The Bible does not deal specifically with abortion, cloning, stem cell research, and *in vitro* fertilization but we can use it and must use it to determine morality. "It is not in man who walks to direct his own steps" (Jeremiah 10:23). Scientific knowledge can be combined with spiritual knowledge to determine this. James 1:5 states, "If any man lacks wisdom, he is to ask of God." Wisdom is the application of knowledge and spiritual wisdom is the spiritual application of such. Determining what is "ethical" is determining what is right or wrong and this involves the use of biblical principles in our application to modern science. With these thoughts in mind, let's now look at God's Word.

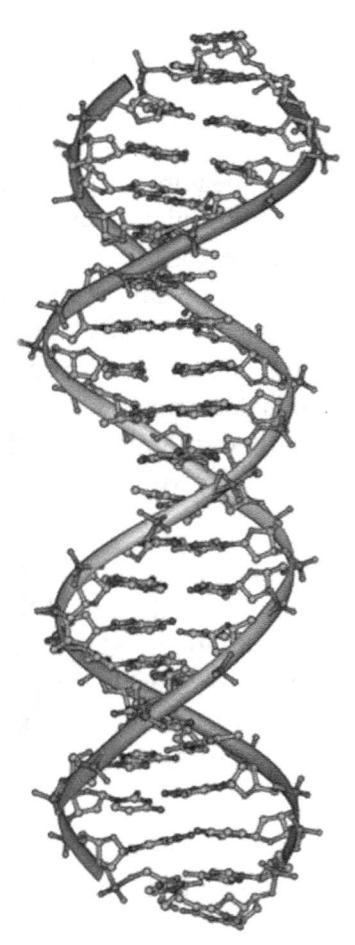

To be sure, God is the creator of the Universe and all its creation and is also the giver of life. David, the Psalmist, in Psalm 24:1 proclaims, "The earth is the Lord's and all it contains, the world and those who dwell in it." Genesis 2:7 states, "God breathed into his [man's] nostrils the breath of life and man became a living being." God chose a most amazing and remarkable vehicle for life—DNA. All life is made of DNA. Plants, bacteria, insects, birds, mammals, and humans are all designed using this complex yet simple molecule discovered by James Watson and Francis Crick in 1953. Dr.

Introduction – A Historical Perspective

Francis Collins, head of the Human Genome Project, has called DNA the "language of God." Though we "share" this molecule with all life forms, there is something very unique about human life. Of human life only did God say he was made "in our own image," referring to the Trinity. How so? Certainly, God does not have DNA, does He? Does God have hands and feet? Surely, the Holy Spirit is referring to the spiritual nature of man. Only man has a soul. Unlike animals who are born with the breath of life, mankind is endowed with both a living spirit that is mortal and a soul that is immortal (Matthew 10:28). Only man can discern right and wrong. Only man worships God. Man only has the ability or capacity for altruism. Think about it. How does evolution explain man's unique disposition to help his fellow man? And only man has the capacity for self-reflection. Descartes noted centuries ago, "I think therefore I am." These qualities separate man from mere animals and were placed there by God. One needs only to look at Jesus' examples of the Good Samaritan in Luke 10 to understand this.

The uniqueness of man can also be seen in his supreme creative ability. The works of Beethoven, Mozart, DaVinci, and countless others attests to the creative ability of man. But God has also given Man the ability to think and reason. Indeed, God's omniscience is manifested in His handiwork to which Psalms 19:11 alludes.

Since God is the giver of human life and human life is unique, one principle we must obey is honoring that human life and not destroying the innocent. This principle is seen throughout the Bible. One of the Ten Commandments is "Thou Shall not Kill" and refers to the taking of innocent life. Cain was banned from Eden for the killing of his innocent brother, Abel. Jesus warns about the taking of innocent life, as do the apostles through the Holy Spirit. The taking of innocent blood or life is, therefore, the bedrock on which we must decide ethical concerns. Another key concept determining morality is the Golden Rule stated by Jesus in Matthew 7:12. We are to treat others as we would want ourselves treated. That is why it is so vitally important to determine when personhood begins.

There are many passages in both the New and Old Testaments where the word "conception" or the idea of "being pregnant" is used, the first being Genesis 4:1. Here Eve is said to have conceived after having relations, a euphemism for sexual intercourse, with Adam. This same Hebrew word *harah*, is used many more times throughout the Old Testament and means to "receive or become full or pregnant."

In the New Testament, the Greek word *gennao*, is used to convey the meaning of conception or pregnancy and basically means the same thing as the Hebrew word *harah*. The Holy Sprit chose this word to describe what occurred to Mary, the mother of Jesus, in Matthew 1:20.

In Luke 1:24, the Greek word *sullambano*, is used to describe the condition of Elizabeth and is translated in the New American Standard, "pregnant." Also in referring to Rebecca, the New Testament uses the word *koiten* translated "conceived" to describe her condition. All these words basically describe the condition of the womb and refer to the state of being "full" or "pregnant or the process of becoming pregnant." This should not be thought of as referring to fertilization since these words do not mean that. We must be true to their meaning. The process we know as "fertilization" is just not found in the Bible.

The Bible does, however, allude to the development that occurs in the womb. Deuteronomy 7:13 refers to the "fruit of the womb." Job says he was "made by God in the womb" (31:15). The Preacher of Ecclesiastes 11:5 proclaims, bones are formed in the womb. Psalms 139:13-16, is perhaps the most eloquent:

> For Thou didst form my inward parts; Thou didst weave me in my mother's womb. I will give thanks to Thee for I am fearfully and wonderfully made; wonderful are Thy works, and my soul knows it very well. My frame was not hidden from Thee, When I was made in secret, and skillfully wrought in the depths of earth. Thine eyes have seen my unformed substance; and in Thy book they were written, the days that were ordained for me when as yet there was not one of them.

These passages show that personhood begins before birth. This is also evident in the New Testament. Luke 1:41 states, "And it came about that when Elizabeth heard Mary's greeting, the baby [John] leaped in her womb; and Elizabeth was filled the Holy Spirit." The text indicates Luke, the physician, through the Holy Spirit, believed a six-month-old "fetus" was a human being. In fact, the text refers to the unborn John as a "baby" and Elizabeth says, "the baby leaped in my womb for joy" showing the baby in the womb has the ability to react to external stimuli.

Other passages could be cited, but all these attest to the belief that a caring and loving God is working to form human beings in the womb. They do not, however, attest to exactly when the precise stage of embryonic development begins or when personhood starts. These passages are not discourses in human embryology but poetically describe the great gift of life God has granted to us and to the beauty of our development and growth which obviously occurs in our mother's womb.

Today several views prevail as to when personhood occurs. No one would argue personhood begins before fertilization though spermatozoons and ovum are certainly human life. The two extreme positions are personhood begins with fertilization and the other is personhood begins at birth or even months later. At this point, we must define "personhood." "Personhood" is not necessarily the beginning of life but instead can be deferred. Clearly, once fertilization takes place, the human sperm and egg cease to exist as distinct entities. A new individual cell now exists called a *zygote* that has the potential of becoming *a* human person. But it also has the potential for other things, as we shall see in the next chapter. Norman Ford in his eloquent book *When Did I Begin* has defined a person as "a living individual with human nature that has within itself the capacity to maintain or at least begin the processes of the human life cycle without loss of identity." In other words, the human person has the active potential to develop towards human adulthood without ceasing to be the same individual. The question is when does this begin?

Let us for the moment, for the sake of debate, take the position that personhood begins sometime after fertilization. Some have argued personhood begins when blood appears in the embryo. Those taking this position turn to Leviticus 17:11, "For the life of the flesh is in the blood" and verse 14, "For the life of all flesh, its blood is identified with life." This concept is reiterated by the apostles in Acts 15:29, prohibiting Christians from eating blood. If this rationale is sound, personhood begins at about the third week after fertilization when the heartbeat of the fetus begins. Another position, and the one held by the Supreme Court of the United States in *Roe v. Wade*, holds that human personhood begins between the fifteenth and twenty-second week of gestation. This is argued from the point of view that a "person" is one who can survive outside the womb. Those taking this position also point out that the fetus does not become truly neurologically active until the fifth month. This coincides with the event known as "quickening" when the fetus begins active neuromuscular activity. Obviously, from our definition of personhood, the unique individual person has already been in existence prior to this. Finally, some Jewish traditions or law, the *Halacha* defines a person when "the baby's head emerges from the wound" or in the breech delivery, personhood begins when most of the body is outside the mother. Modern Jewish belief holds the fetus in great value and abortion is not permitted on genetic grounds but only if the mother's life is in danger. Nonetheless, the fetus does not gain full humanity until birth. Those taking this position point to Exodus 21:22-23. This passage deals with the accidental injury to a pregnant woman. If the woman dies, the penalty is life for life; if she miscarries, the guilty party is merely fined. Once again, in this situation, given our definition of personhood, the individual has already existed.

Before leaving our discussion of personhood, it is necessary to discuss at least one alternative view, albeit a very controversial and perverse one, yet one accepted by many, if not most current bioethicists and philosophers, especially those in the reproductive sciences. Borrowing from the eighteenth century philosopher John Locke, Peter Singer, the chair of the tenured position of the Center for Human Values at Princeton University, and one of the most influential philosophers and bioethicists of our time, defines "personhood" as "having the possession of traits like the capacity to feel and reason, self awareness and autonomy and the ability to imagine a future. For personhood to exist, an individual then must have a completely developed and normally functioning cerebral cortex." *Sentience*, which means the capacity to have experiences and react to external stimuli and the capacity for self-awareness and self-consciousness, is deemed a requirement for personhood. With this definition, Mr. Singer, the world's foremost proponent of utilitarianism, assigns personhood *after* birth. In fact, with his definition, some humans born with severe disabilities never achieve personhood while some non-humans, such as the great apes, do! Needless to say, this extreme position has some very serious ramifications. As a result of this philosophy, the consequences of an action are more important than the intention or motivation behind it. With Singer espousing this philosophy, he argues animals are on the same moral plane with humans because of their ability to feel pain and pleasure. The exploitation of animals is labeled "Speciesism" by Mr. Singer.

Singer values persons over non-persons, even if these persons are animals. Mr. Singer has been quoted as saying, "Killing a disabled infant is not morally equivalent to killing a person. Very often, it is not wrong at all."

Singer believes parents should have up to twenty-eight days after the birth of a child to decide if that child lives or dies based upon its disability. In arguing his point, Mr. Singer sees no difference between killing a child after birth and killing a fetus still in the uterus if that being is to be spared from a life time of pain because of disability. On this subject, Mr. Singer makes a good point, though the problem is both positions are wrong! This is exactly what *Roe v. Wade* has brought us to today. If it is justified to "terminate" a pregnancy, why is it wrong to kill an infant with a disability after it is born, argues Mr. Singer.

Regarding Mr. Singer's philosophy, one question to ask is: Who decides what "disability" is and how severe does that "disability" have to be to justify the killing of an infant child? It would seem from Mr. Singer's writings, the parents ultimately make this decision, although he would establish "very strict conditions" for the permissibility of infanticide. Clearly, Mr. Singer's position is contrary to biblical teaching and he sees nothing "sacred" in human life.

Mr. Singer goes on to state, "In order to bring about the greater good of society, the term personhood can be removed from an individual with severe disabilities such as those in a comatose state or those with severe dementia." As a result, killing such an individual is not the moral equivalent of killing a person and, therefore, not morally wrong! Again, the question is: Who determines when a person becomes a non-person? Certainly, medical "experts" frequently underestimate the quality of life experienced by people with disabilities and, therefore, should not be relied on to answer such questions, even though Singer believes doctors can identify "persons" with little doubt. Obviously, this is all very disconcerting and resembles too much the despicable philosophy of the Third Reich! The paradox of Mr. Singer's philosophy is that his parents were Viennese Jews who escaped the Holocaust, and three of his grandparents died in Nazi concentration camps. Though Singer protests such analogies to Nazism, his philosophy reeks of eugenics, *Mein Kampf*, and Dr. Josef Mengele.

Lest you think Mr. Singer's philosophy is a minority opinion, keep in mind he is joined by other eminent influential philosophers such as Jonathan Glove and John Harris, who hold similar philosophical beliefs. He is also the Ira W. DeCamp Professor of Bioethics at Princeton, Laureate Professor at the Center of Applied Philosophy and Public Ethics at the University of

Melbourne, and in 2004 was named the Australian humanist of the year. He is a prolific writer and has published numerous papers and books, including: *Animal Liberation, Practical Ethics,* and *Rethinking Life and Death.* He has been labeled "the most influential philosopher of the world today." Diane Coleman, President of "NOT DEAD YET," an organization dedicated to the protection of human rights for the disabled, has called Mr. Singer "the most dangerous man in the world today." She points out that, through his published works and teaching positions at Princeton and Harvard Medical Schools, Mr. Singer is "advocating public policy that would deprive millions with cognitive disabilities equal protection of the law and allow those who do not meet his fuzzy criteria for personhood to be killed by medical professionals with the consent of their families."

Utilitarnism philosophy is gaining ground and, as stated earlier, may even be the most popular philosophy amongst bioethicists today. Whether consciously or not, our society seems to be accepting the definition of personhood visa vie our acceptance of abortion, and in some cases late term abortion. Nonetheless, Mr. Singer's ethics and morality are deplorable and need to be rebuked. With his cry of "speciesism" he has merely replaced one form of "discrimination" with another, that of "cortical function." His definition of personhood leads to silly scenarios. For example, if one lapses into a temporary comatose state, has that individual now become a non-person? Clearly, an individual's moral values and significance should not depend on the vagaries of their central nervous system function.

In deference to Mr. Singer, humans are different from animals. A child is a person long before he is born and does not have to earn his personhood by demonstrating cognitive abilities. God has given us life and all human life must be treated with dignity and respect, no matter how tragically incapacitated that life is. It is love that separates man from animals manifested in God's love towards us and our love towards our fellow man. When we were born, we were totally dependent on our parents and many of us, in later life, will no doubt be dependent on our children or others for our well-being. Expressing our love to one another validates our humanity and is one way we demonstrate the image of God, of which we are made. Shame on Peter Singer and shame on Princeton University for placing him in such a prominent position.

At this point, we are still left with identifying when personhood begins.

To further answer this question, a brief look at human embryology is necessary. In the next chapter, we will do just that; after which, we will turn out attention once again to the question of personhood.

Chapter 2
Embryology – Determining Personhood

I will give thanks to Thee, for I am fearfully and wonderfully made . . . (Psalms 139:14).

Our discussion of Christian Ethics and medical science as addressed in the previous chapter, of necessity involves the determination of personhood and when it begins. A basic understanding of embryology is, therefore, necessary. What follows will be a brief discussion of human embryology with emphasis on fertilization and early fetal development. Textbooks are written on embryology, so obviously we will not be able to go into great detail. Nonetheless, an elemental understanding of this subject is mandatory in an attempt to identify the beginning of personhood.

Before discussing fertilization or syngamy, we must first look at gametogenesis. "Mitosis" refers to the process that results in cellular division or duplication, which occurs in the somatic cells of our bodies. Mitosis will also be involved in the rapid growth of the fertilized ovum. Mitosis starts with forty-six chromosomes (a diploid cell) and duplicates itself with two new diploid cells. Under normal circumstances, a diploid cell cannot "grow" into a human individual, although all the genetic material to do so is there within the cell nucleus. Cloning techniques have been able to overcome this obstacle, however.

"Gametogenesis," on the other hand, involves a process known as meiosis and occurs in the testes of the male and in the ovaries of the female. Through this process, the normal diploid cells with 46 chromosomes will be transformed into gametocytes, which are haploid, containing 23 chromosomes in the sperm and the ovum. For our purposes, we will be discussing the normal or typical process of fertilization with some very brief points regarding abnormal fertilization.

The male gametocyte, that is the sperm, will undergo two meiotic divisions, resulting in four haploid cells, two with X chromosomes and two with Y chromosomes. The average male produces billions of sperm during his lifetime and, during coitus, the male ejaculates an average of 2-3 million sperm, half of which contain the Y chromosome and the other half the X chromosome. In essence, the male sperm determines the sexuality of the ensuing zygote, although the ovum may have some "influence." Oogenesis,

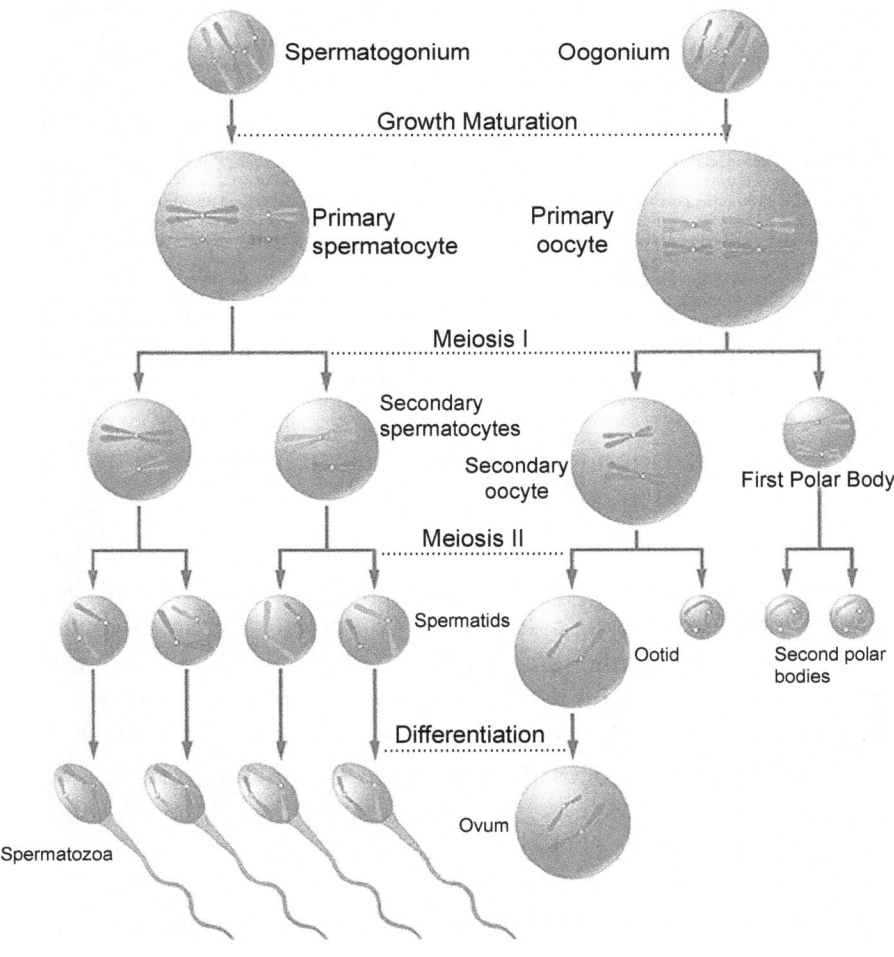

or the production of the ovocyte, or ovum, is somewhat different. During the first meiotic division, one oocyte is formed with a haploid number of chromosomes, 23; the other "cell" produced becomes the first polar body of the ovocyte, or ovum. At ovulation, which occurs at the tenth through fourteenth day of the menstrual cycle, the ovum is released into the fallopian, or uterine, tube of the female. It is not until the beginning of fertilization that the ovum goes through its second meiotic division and the second polar body is produced.

Fertilization under normal circumstances takes place in the fallopian tubes of the female. Again, normally, only one ovum is released at ovulation by just one of the ovaries. If more than one ovum is released, the possibility of dizygotic twinning (that is non-identical or paternal twinning) exists. Fertilization proceeds after intercourse when a certain number of sperm make their way through the uterus to the fallopian tube and to the ovum, which is encased by a group of cells known as the zona pellucida. Although several sperm will attach to the zona pellucida, normally only one sperm will penetrate and enter the ovum. The other sperm may aid in the break down of the zona pellucida but do not enter the ovum. This process is called capacitation. If more than one sperm does penetrate into the ovum, the resultant fertilization either never develops fully or the baby dies at childbirth due to the significant aberration formed. During capacitation, only the "head" of the sperm, which contains its 23 chromosomes, enters the ovum with its tail and shell left behind. It is now that the ovum goes through its second meiotic division to produce another polar body. Note that if either polar body is fertilized, which is sometimes the case, the zygote does not usually develop.

At this point, we now have an ovum, which contains 46 chromosomes. Before any mingling of chromosomes occurs, the original 23 from both the male and the female form what are called pronuclei. Once this happens, the two pronuclei come together and finally the 46 chromosomes line up in 23 pairs and we have the beginning of a new entity, which is neither the sperm nor the egg. This new entity is referred to as the zygote and its "life" is very short-lived. The whole process leading up to the production of the zygote takes up to 24 hours and occurs in the proximal portion of the fallopian tube called the "infundibulum." The first mitotic division, known as cleavage, marks the end of the zygote and results in two new cells that are referred to as the embryo, though a better term might be the "pre-embryo" or possibly the "pro-embryo." This definition of "pre-embryo" has been suggested by the American Fertility Society Ethics Committee to describe the entity formed at the end-process of fertilization up until the single primitive streak occurs, which will be discussed later. After fertilization, very quickly, multiple cleavages occur through the mitotic process, eventually producing a mass of cells that is grape-like in appearance and referred to as the "morula." During the early phases of the cleavage process, each individual cell is totipotent. This means that each individual cell with its 46 chromosomes, separated from the other cells, has the potential of becoming an individual by itself, containing all the genetic material necessary to develop into a human being. They also have the potential to transform into many germ lines. These are "stem cells." At this time, however, there is no differentiation going on. The morula is now in the isthmus of the fallopian or uterine tubes at about the third day after the beginning of fertilization.

The next stage of development is the "blastocyte," which occurs at about the fourth or fifth day. The blastocyte has an inner cell mass, a fluid-filled cavity, and an outer cell mass made up of a very thin layer of cells destined to become trophoblasts, which will make up the placenta. By now, the blastocyte is floating freely in the uterine cavity but beginning to attach by the sixth day to the posterior wall of the uterus, the usual site of implantation. Some cellular specification and differentiation is beginning to take place by way of the trophoblast, with the embryoblast not yet differentiating. At this stage, trophoblasts dominate and begin to attach to the uterine wall in order to nourish the subsequent embryo. Once this occurs, the embryoblast begins to differentiate. (See figure below.) This remains one of the great enigmas in embryology and indeed medical science. Just what and how differentiation is

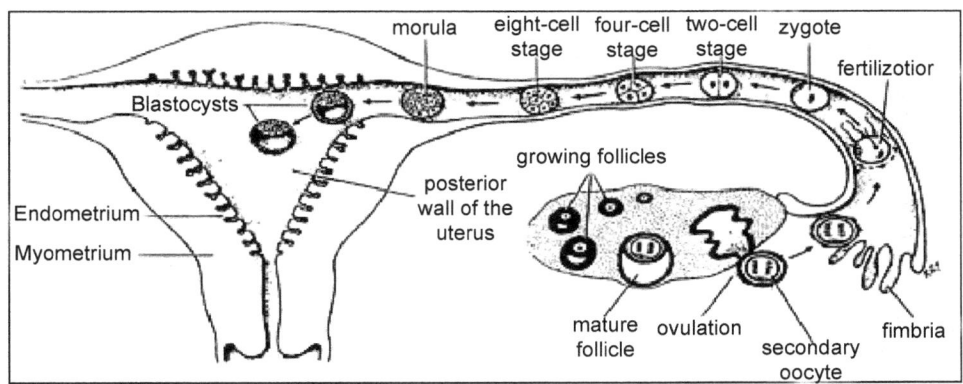

"triggered" in the embryoblast is not known. Spemann and Mangold called this process "organization." We still know virtually nothing about this. Obviously, something "tells" which cells to become heart, skeletal muscle, brain, bone, digestive, reproductive tissue, as well as over 200 other tissue types, but how this occurs, as stated, remains a great mystery. Once cells become differentiated, there is no going back to other kinds of tissue.

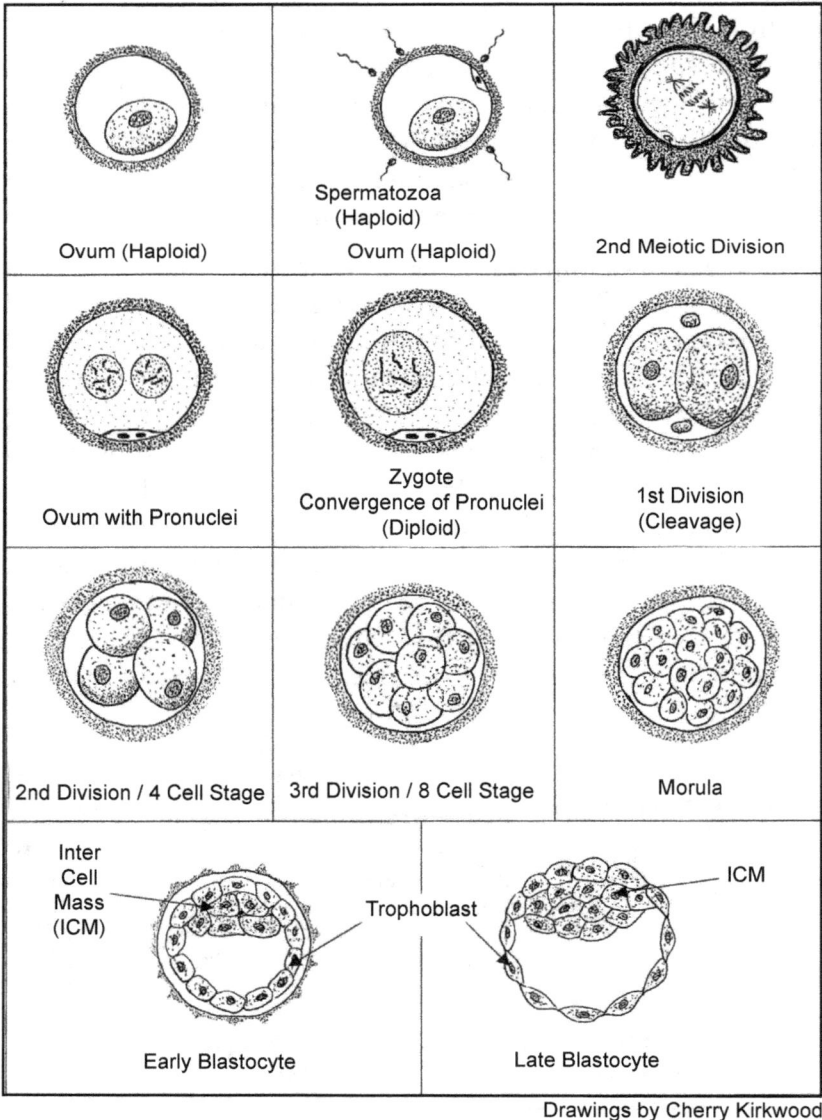

Drawings by Cherry Kirkwood

Implantation is then completed by the end of the second week of embryonic development. It is now that the embryo becomes bilaminar with the development of the embryonic disc that gives rise to germ layers, which will form all the tissues and organs of the embryo. After implantation in about the end of the third week, the embryo has formed a trilaminar disc in the beginning of what is referred to as the "primitive streak." In some cases of fertilization, a primitive streak is never formed and the embryo proper does not develop, though the placenta will continue. This is called a "blighted ovum" or a failed fertilization. Blighted ovum occur commonly with "*in vitro*" fertilization, hence is one of the reasons multiple fertilized ovum are placed in the uterus during *in vitro* fertilization. If a "primitive streak" does develop, it is at this point when cells are committed to be either the embryo proper or extra-embryonic membranes. After this stage, monozygotic, or identical twinning, can no longer develop. According to Dr. Ford, "the appearance of the 'primitive streak' signals that only one embryo proper and one individual has been formed and begun to exist." Before this point, the developing embryo was a mass of "loosely" organized cells developing into a variety of tissues waiting for the "clock" of development to occur that would synchronize and trigger human development into a single human individual.

Once differentiation begins, the development of various organs of the human body is rapid. Rudiments of a heart appear during the third week of development. The early eye appears at the twenty-fifth day. By day thirty-two, hands and feet are beginning to develop and by the sixty-sixth day, the face of the developing baby has a distinctive human appearance. Finally, by the seventieth day of development, all organs including external genitalia are formed and the rest of the time in the womb is spent in maturation, development and growth until the 40th week. (See figure on next page.). Up to the twenty-second to twenty-third week of gestation, the infant is still not mature enough, especially pulmonary wise, to survive outside of the mother's womb. After the twenty-third week, an infant can survive with the help of modern neonatal care. Admittedly, the above discussion is simplistic and apologies are given to those desirous of more detail. We are aware that much, much more is involved. Nevertheless, these basics will help in the following discussions pertaining to personhood.

Determining Personhood

Many would argue personhood begins at fertilization and there are some

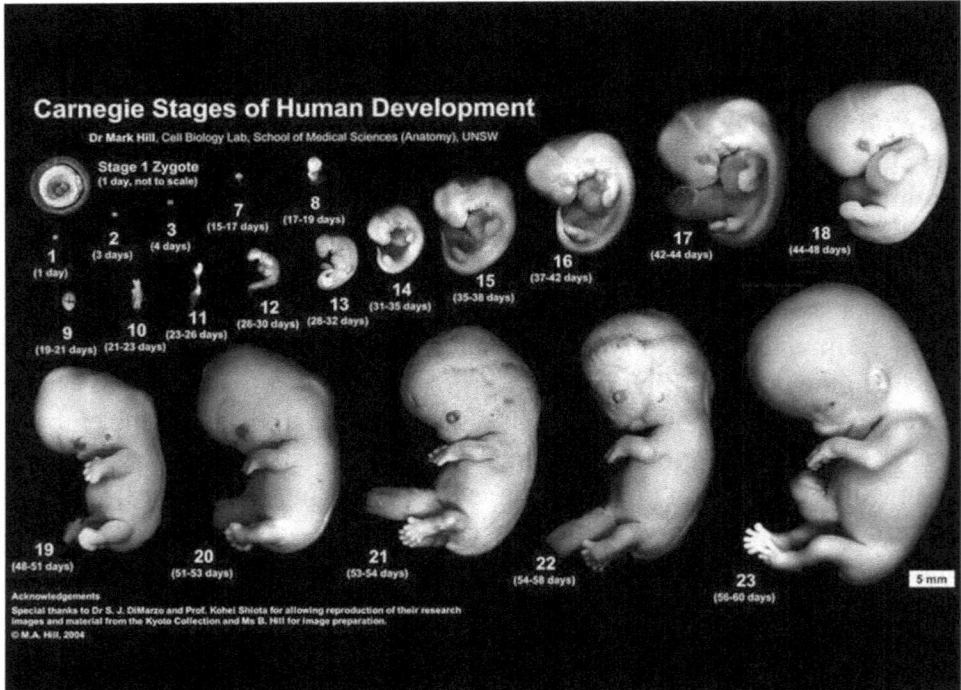

compelling reasons for their beliefs. First, and perhaps foremost, the completion of the fertilization process, which joins two haploid cells and gives rise to a single diploid zygote contains genetic material for the complete development of a human individual. Notwithstanding monozygotic twins, this genetic material is unique for each individual. If all goes well under "normal circumstances" after multiple cleavages, growth, and development, a new human infant will be the result. A second argument for personhood beginning at fertilization is that the developing embryo maintains the capacity for self-direction and organizes its own self-maintenance and self development in many aspects. The exact process for this is poorly understood but a fertilized ovum should not be thought of as a tiny human being that develops into a full person, which is preformationism, discussed in Chapter 1. Fertilization then is the most important biological stage in the process of human life and of this, there can be doubt. So there are compelling reasons to believe personhood begins at fertilization and many theologians, scholars, and perhaps the majority of the Christian world, take this position. Still the question remains: If personhood does begin at fertilization, at what point in fertilization does it occur? Does it occur when the sperm attaches to the ovum or when the sperm enters the ovum? Maybe it begins when the pronuclei are formed, or perhaps when the pronuclei come together and the 23 chromosomes from the ovum and the sperm unite? Or does it happen when the first cleavage occurs? These are difficult questions but need to be asked nonetheless. Debate still occurs among the scientific community what determines the "end" of fertilization.

There are, however, some problems in fixing "personhood" at fertilization, as we shall see. Dr. Clifford Grobstein has stated, "Rigid and overly simplistic criteria may seem gratifyingly final, but their simplicity often proves illusory when confronted by complex reality." For example, some have said after fertilization, all you have is growth and development. Clearly, the above discussion refutes this inaccuracy. The basic question is: Can personhood begin at fertilization when fertilization can result in more than the formation of one individual? This becomes apparent when looking at the phenomenon of monozygotic twinning that can occur up to the morula stage of development. We do not know what causes monozygotic twinning but it results when the embryo divides. What was one "embryo" now becomes two totally different developing "embryos" and separate individual persons. Dizygotic twinning occurs when two ovum are fertilized by two different sperm, they never share genetic material. Monozygotic twins, on the other hand, share exactly the same DNA, hence they are identical genetically but no one argues they are the same individual. So can we really say that an individual's beginning occurs at fertilization when that process may result later in more than one individual? Monozygotic twinning is a good argument to place personhood at some point other than fertilization.

Then there is the case of the chimera. The word "chimera" comes from an ancient greek mythological character made up of multiple animals. One picture of the chimera shows a creature with two heads, one a lion and the other an antelope, with the body of a goat. (See figure.) In nature, chimeras are formed by the combination of two or more zygotes, which is two or more fertilized eggs. As a result, the individual has a mixture of genetic material from four or more "parent" cells, that is two sperm and two ovum or more. The expression of

genetic material will vary from one individual to another. For example, some chimeras will have different color eyes, one being brown possibly and the other being blue. They may have different types of thumbs with one thumb being a "hitchhiker's thumb," and the other a normal thumb. Tetragametic chimerism is the term for two zygotes fusing together. This usually happens at a very early stage such as the blastocyte stage. If the two zygotes were male and female, hermaphroditism may occur. Interspecies chimeras have been "created" in the lab successfully, using sheep and goats (geep) as well as rats and mice (rice). Human chimeras, once thought to be very rare, may be more common than formerly believed. A chimeric individual may go through life never knowing his chimerism, unless genetic testing is performed. The most famous case of chimerism was that of the Lydia Fairchild incident. In this case, which occurred in 2002, Ms. Fairchild was accused of Welfare fraud in claiming to have children that were proven to not be "genetically hers." It was only through more extensive genetic testing that Ms. Fairchild was found to be a chimera with two sets of genetic material and was exonerated of her accusations. This then begs the question: Can personhood begin at fertilization when two or more zygotes can "fuse together," creating one individual? If so, you would have two persons becoming one! This is quite illogical and chimerism implies personhood must begin sometime after fertilization.

With twinning and chimerism, normal fertilization has taken place with significant changes occurring afterwards. Abnormal fertilization can occur and this also argues against personhood beginning at fertilization. One such case is that of the hydatiform mole, a grape-like cluster of chorionic villi, known about since antiquity. Here, no embryo is formed at all, only placental tissue. The father only contributes to fertilization with 46 chromosomes. This occurs when a single haploid sperm fertilizes an ovum with either no pronuclei or deformed pronuclei. After entering the ovum, the sperm doubles its own chromosomes. As a result, what is called a molar pregnancy ensues. The "mole" is alive and of human origin, but no one would argue that it is an individual.

Teratomas are also the result of fertilization gone wrong. A teratoma is a result of fertilization that causes an uncontrolled growth of cells and tissue that is genetically human but has no potential of becoming truly human or an individual with human nature. It represents a very serious error in the development process and occurs in either the ovary or the testes of a developing infant although it does not necessarily need to attach to either. If it is attached to a gonad, it acts more like a cancerous growth and though the developing fetus is certainly a human individual, the teratoma is clearly not. These are four arguments against personhood beginning at fertilization but still the questions remains: When is the best time to assign personhood? It may be that only God knows the answer to that question precisely. It is certainly our belief that all human tissue should be treated with the utmost respect and dignity. And certainly, the question of ensoulment can only be answered by God. Still, we believe there is a point when logic dictates personhood begins.

Let us look back at the definition of personhood given in the First Chapter. A person is a living individual with human nature that has within itself the capacity to maintain, or at least begin, the processes of the human life cycle without loss of identity. From this definition, the beginning of personhood would seem to occur at the beginning of the "primitive streak." Dr. Howard Jones has stated, "It is only with the appearance of a single primitive streak in the embryoblast that one is guaranteed that a single biologic individual is in the process of formation from the pre-embryo." With the development of the "primitive streak," the fetus is now a single entity and although abnormalities can develop, these abnormalities will not result in twinning, chimerism, teratomas or hydatiform moles. The infant may be born with serious problems and other abnormalities, but he or she will be a person or individual.

To delay assigning personhood at a later time, we believe, is wrong and would violate moral and ethical principles from a biblical standpoint, the reasons for which we were given in Chapter 1. Certainly, just because a baby would not survive outside the womb does not take away his personhood. A full-term baby left on its own will not survive for long, yet we are all appalled when we read in newspapers about some abandoned infant. Also, we believe abortion to be an abomination. Abortion violates the principle of "shedding innocent blood." Dr. Grobstein, in his book *Science and the Unborn* has stated, "In terms of maternal effect, therefore, pregnancy begins not with conception but with implantation. Implantation may be thought of as the physiologic beginning of actual maternal pregnancy as well as the offspring's significance depending on its mother."

One may ask: Is assigning personhood an important point? Practically speaking, maybe not, but as witnessed from our previous chapter, philosophically, it certainly is. Certainly, a woman does not realize she is pregnant until the beginning of the primitive streak when attachment to the uterine wall occurs and when hormones are produced and can be measured, indicating pregnancy in the womb. This is also when a woman notices the "feelings" of pregnancy and her menstruation usually stops. All this can coincide at about the time, again, when the primitive streak appears. Furthermore, with the exception of the RU-486 pill (or the abortion pill), other forms of birth control affect fertilization before this point in time and even the morning-after pill, which will be discussed in Chapter 5, works primarily by preventing ovulation. An abortion would not be considered prior to this point as the woman would not realize her pregnancy as of yet.

Placing personhood at fertilization has some philosophical problems too. It is estimated between 20 and 50% of all pregnancies result in spontaneous abortion or miscarriage. In most cases, the woman never knew fertilization had taken place. Placing personhood at this stage would mean God has assigned personhood to fertilized eggs of which 20-50% of them never achieve implantation. This just doesn't make sense. Is most of heaven made up of individuals of less than three weeks gestation? Maybe it is not coincidental that Luke states in Chapter 2 of his Gospel, conception occurs in the womb. Completed implantation and the "primitive streak" occur at about the same time. We think there may be some solace to be found in realizing personhood begins later than fertilization and there are no biblical principles broken or ignored by this concept.

Chapter 3
Cloning
By Dr. Ron Kirkwood

And in your seed (Abraham) all the nations of the earth shall be blessed because you have obeyed my voice (Genesis 22:18).

And Isaac prayed to the Lord on behalf of his wife, because she was barren; and the Lord answered him and Rebekah his wife conceived. But the children struggled together within her; and she said, "If it is so, why then am I this way?" So she went to inquire of the Lord. And the Lord said to her: "Two nations are in your womb; and two peoples shall be separated from your body; and one people shall be stronger than the other; and the older shall serve the younger." When her days to be delivered were fulfilled, behold, there were twins in her womb. Now the first came forth red, all over like a hairy garment; and they called him Esau. And afterward his brother came forth with his hand holding on Esau's heel, so his name was called Jacob; and Isaac was sixty years old when she gave birth to them. When the boys grew up Esau became a skillful hunter, a man of the field; but Jacob was a peaceful man, living in tents (Genesis 25:21-27).

I begin this chapter on cloning with the above scripture recording the birth of twins. Cloning does occur naturally; identical twins are clones. The chances of a pregnancy producing identical twins are one in 285. Identical, or monozygotic, twins develop when a single egg or oocytes is fertilized by a single sperm. These twins share identical genetic makeup and monozygotic twins are always the same gender, except in extremely rare cases of chromosomal defects. Identical twins look similar but may have many differences. Identical twins do not run in families and genetic factors do not have much, if any affect, on the incidence of identical twins.

Non-identical twins, also known as fraternal twins, are genetically no different than two siblings born at different times. Fraternal, or dizygotic, multiples are formed when two separate eggs or oocytes are fertilized by two separate sperm. It is not unusual to have different genders with the birth of fraternal twins. Fraternal twins do run in families. A female fraternal twin has a one in seventeen chance of giving birth to her own set of twins. The incidence of fraternal twin births is affected by many factors including the quality of medical care and good nutrition. The time of year and where a person lives affects the numbers of twin births as well. As one might expect, the use of fertility drugs and IVF (*in vitro* fertilization) has increased the rate of fraternal twinning.

Esau and Jacob are an example of non-identical or fraternal twins. Esau was red and his skin like a hairy garment. Jacob's appearance is not given to us. We are also told that Esau developed skills as a hunter and was a man of the field and that Jacob was a mild man who dwelled in tents. Esau and Jacob are no different than any other fraternal twins and genetically they are no different than any other brother or sister that would be born at different times. Their chromosomes and DNA are different.

Identical twins like clones have exactly the same chromosomes containing the same DNA and are the result of the splitting of one fertilized egg by one sperm. At the time of fertilization the egg and sperm unite to form a zygote. Identical twins are formed when, for reasons that are not completely understood, the zygote, after the first division into two blastomeres, does not continue to divide in one unit but splits into two units each containing one identical blastomere. The result are two distinct individuals. Only about 32% of identical twins are the result of division at the two blastomere stage. Division into two identical twins can begin even after the two blastomere stage and up to twelve days after fertilization. Conjoined twins also known, as Siamese twins are a result of late division. Identical twins are born about 4000 times each day. We do not completely understand why monozygotic twinning (identical twins) takes place.

It is important to note that fraternal twins do not have the same chromosomes and thus, not the same DNA. Identical twins do have the same chromosomes and same DNA. This is why identical twins look so much alike. Why don't identical twins look exactly the same and why don't they have the same emotional makeup and IQ? Part of the answer to these questions has to do with the expression of genes that make up the chromosomes. The environment plays an important role in developing our personalities. Where we live, social, and cultural values help to make us who we are.

In 1978 a fictional movie entitled *The Boys from Brazil* was released which starred Gregory Peck, Sir Lawrence Olivier, James Mason, and Steve Guttenberg. It is the story of a young Nazi hunter that had gone to Paraguay in the late 1970's to find the famous Nazi physician Josef Mengele, the man responsible for carrying out eugenic and medical experiments on prisoners in Nazi concentration camps. Mysteriously, 65-year-old civil servant men are being killed all over the world. Steve Guttenberg is the young Nazi hunter that stumbles upon the secret that Dr. Mengele has orchestrated all these murders. Each one of these more than ninety men who were murdered had a young boy living with the family. It turns out that each of these young boys was cloned from the blood of Adolf Hitler obtained by Dr. Mengele before Hitler's death. In order to have a better chance of creating another Fuehrer, the boys had been placed in an environment that approximated that which a young Hitler had experienced. Hitler's father had been a civil servant and was killed around his 65th birthday. The reason for the murders is discovered and Mengele's plot to have another leader like Hitler is quashed.

In 1993 the film *Jurassic Park* was released. Cloning again is used in the setting of an isolated island where dinosaurs have been cloned. In the movie, some of the creatures cloned were done so from DNA found in blood that had been preserved in a mosquito. One of the characters in the film is played by Jeff Goldblum who, in one of the scenes discussing cloning, states, "I think too many people were too busy asking if we could clone dinosaurs instead of asking if we should."

The above accounts were fictional, but in February 1997 the first mammal from an adult body (somatic) cell was successfully cloned by a group of veterinary researchers/scientists in Edinburg, Scotland. Ian Wilmut and his colleagues at the Roslin Institue led the work. A process called somatic cell nuclear transfer was used to clone Dolly, a young lamb. This procedure required removing an egg or oocyte from a Scottish Blackface ewe, a type of sheep that has a black face, and then removing the nucleus from that egg. A mammary gland cell was then removed from a mature type of sheep called a Finn Dorset that is all white. The nucleus from the mammary gland cell was then implanted in the egg taken from the Scottish Blackface ewe.

Prior to implantation of the nucleus of the mammary gland, Wilmut starved the mammary cells for five days before extracting the nucleus as this was thought to cause the cells to go into a quiescent phase that would make them more likely to be accepted by the egg. An electrical current was then introduced and the new egg, with the nucleus from the mammary gland, after several division of cells were noted, was implanted into the womb of the Scottish Blackface ewe. After 148 days, the normal gestation time for sheep, Dolly was born. It took 277 somatic cell nuclear transfers to produce the single viable Dolly. The success of Dolly is in finally demonstrating that a cell from a specialized organ like a mammary gland could have all the genetic information contained in the chromosomes of that cell reprogrammed to grow an entire organism.

The rest of this chapter will answer the questions: What is cloning and how does it or can it affect me as a Christian? A strict definition of cloning is the genetic copying of all of the DNA or entire genome of an organism. All life has genomes. Both plants and animals have distinct genomes. Human genomes are made up of the chromosomes in each cell's nucleus as well as the chromosomes of the mitochondria in the cytoplasm. Most cloning today is done by somatic cell nuclear transfer, the same technique that was used to clone Dolly. The only way to produce an exact clone would be to clone the egg donor with her own somatic (body) cell since genetic material is always in the mitochondria in the cytoplasm. Dolly is not an exact clone for this reason. No male can be an exact clone using this method of cloning.

There are basically three different types of cloning. There is recombinant DNA technology or DNA cloning, reproductive cloning, and therapeutic cloning. I will not spend time on DNA cloning. This is a method to clone fragments of DNA or a gene and may be helpful in eventually curing a multiple number of diseases.

Reproductive cloning is a technology that can use either somatic cell nuclear transfer techniques or specialized splitting techniques also called artificial twinning. The goal of reproductive cloning is to reproduce an animal or human with the same DNA as the other. This is already being done commercially. Recently the news revealed that the Otto family who live in Florida had paid $155,000 to a California based company, working in South Korea, for the cloning of their deceased Labrador retriever. The couple's dog had died from cancer about one year prior to it being cloned. The couple now has a puppy that looks exactly like their former pet. The couple said that they realized that there is no guarantee that this puppy will have the same disposition or character of their former pet.

Scientists have cloned mice from somatic cells that were collected from mice that had been dead and frozen for sixteen years. An endangered wild sheep has been cloned. Horses have been cloned. Many different kinds of animals have been cloned since Dolly. It is now theoretically possible to clone humans.

Therapeutic cloning not only is linked to the generation of early embryos for stem cell research but is also concerned with the developing of technologies that might benefit man for organ transplant. The word used to describe the transplantation of animal organs into humans is "xenotransplantation." Pigs have already been cloned. It is thought that one-day pig organs through cloning techniques may overcome the problem with human rejection so that people with kidney failure might have a kidney from a cloned pig that would not require anti-rejection medications to suppress the human immune system response to a foreign protein. Pigs produce a special sugar called alpha 1,3 galactose, which human immune cells target. The key to preventing rejection is to remove the gene or genes that create an enzyme that transfers this special sugar to the surface of the cells. This was accomplished by scientist working with PPL Therapeutics, a British biotechnology company, in August 2002. They have created what is called "double knock-out" pigs. These are pigs that have been genetically engineered to lack both copies of a gene, which causes the human immune response to reject the transplant. There are continued fears that as a result of transplanting pig organs into humans, pig viruses could enter into the human population.

There is now the ability to use what is called "cytoplasmic hybrids" (also known as "cybrids") to clone humans. This technique would use a cow's egg that is enucleated and the nucleus then replaced with a somatic cell nucleus from a human. This zygote could then be developed and specialized cells could be programmed to grow a human kidney, liver, etc. The first human hybrid clone was created in November 1998 when a human cell and a cow's egg were used for somatic cell nuclear transfer. It was destroyed after twelve days. The director of the program stated that the embryo could not be thought of as human since an embryo is not normally implanted into the uterus until around fourteen days,

There is research going on with parthenogenetic embryos. Basically this is taking a human egg and stimulating it chemically so that it will begin to divide to form embryonic tissue, just as if a sperm had fertilized it, in order to produce organs for transplantation as well as medical research. Since no sperm was used to create this embryonic tissue, some would argue it would not be truly human and the thinking is that fewer would object to this technique to create stem cells for research.

There are lots of questions to answer as a Christian concerning cloning. I am sure, as time goes forward, many will be confronted on a personal level about issues concerning cloning. A few years ago a California couple discovered that their daughter was dying from leukemia. The father had a reversal of a vasectomy and the mother became pregnant at forty-three to have a child for the primary purpose of providing bone marrow for bone marrow transplantation in order to save the older sister. Many think that it would be much easier to clone the daughter with leukemia and produce the bone marrow needed for transplant.

Another possible scenario would be the following: A thirty-five year-old man is left sterile as a result of medical treatment for lymphoma at sixteen years of age. He and his wife would like to have children. He would like to take a somatic cell from himself and use one of his wife's eggs to clone a son. This son would be no different genetically than the man; it would be as if the child was his identical twin. There would obviously have to be the technical skills to correct for any problems associated with the mother's DNA in the cytoplasm. There are lots of ethical questions to consider with this situation. For example, the father is genetically the brother to this child as well as his father.

And yet another example: A little girl just a few weeks shy of her seventh birthday falls out of a window on the second floor of her house. The parents are devastated by the death and cannot talk about it for months. They want to have another child. They want to clone their deceased daughter. The parents realize that the clone will not be their first child. They realize that, by cloning, all they will get is a child that is an identical twin of their deceased daughter. "We think of the clone as her twin or at least a baby that will look like her." Personality is not only related to our genetic coding but is highly dependent on social feedback. Even birth order has an effect on our personalities.

Every cell in our body carries the genetic coding for our entire physical makeup. The color of our hair, eyes, the shape of our nose, the size of our ears and our height are all programmed in our DNA. Our genetic information has a lot to do with what we are. However, we cannot downplay the effects our environment, culture, and society play in forming who we are. Genetically identical individuals do not equal identical human beings.

Our liver does what a liver normally does because of its programmed specialization. What happens during the process of fetal development is cells that initially have the potential to become anything begin to be encoded to perform special functions. Some of the cells become brain tissue, some of the cells become bone, and some of the cells become other tissues. Each of these specialized cells is encoded to do what they do by their genetic material, DNA, being either "turned on or turned off." All the functions performed are because of its direction in each cell that forms this organ. The significance of Dolly and all the cloned animals since then is that we now know that each specialized cell has the ability to be stimulated in such a way that a total organism can be created that contains the distinct genetic material from the individual that produced that cell. It has been shown with the right stimulus that even a liver cell can have its programming altered to the point that an entirely new being can be formed from that one cell.

In October 1993, Jerry Hall, the director of the *in vitro* lab at George Washington University, along with his partner Dr. Robert Stillman, head of the entire *in vitro* program to the American Fertility Society in Montreal, Canada, presented a paper that showed that they were able to start with seventeen microscopic embryos and by a process of splitting were able to multiply that number to forty-eight. A furor arose over the paper. Stillman reassured everyone that the work was a modest scientific advance that might someday prove useful for treating certain types of infertility. In an interview with Larry King, Jerry Hall stated, "We have set out to provide some basic information. It is up to the ethicist and medical community, with input from the general public, to decide what kind of guidelines will lead us in the future."

We live in a technologically advancing time. *In vitro* fertilization was effectively illegal in many states up until twenty years ago. The idea of a heart transplant was unimaginable not that long ago. Cloning and stem cell research will affect our lives in the future.

There will be many questions that each of us as Christians will have to answer concerning cloning. Normally, we are each the product of our parents. We have half of or forty-six chromosomes from our father and the other half from our mother. We are not who we are simply because of our genes. Each of us has a soul. We are all created in the image of God. Each has free moral will. Each has the right to choose. We are not just the pinnacle of the Animal Kingdom.

I have lots of questions myself. I believe in the providence of God. I don't know exactly how that works. I do know that Joseph was only able to see how it worked in his life after the fact. I believe that God has given us a brain to use and each one of us will have to answer specific questions as they arise. Here is what we can take to the bank. Any individual human being whether created in the traditional way through sexual intercourse, *in vitro* fertilization, or by cloning will have a soul and will be accountable to God.

Chapter 4
Stem Cell Research
By John Kirkwood

Before I formed you in the womb I knew you, and before you were born I consecrated you; I have appointed you a prophet to the nations (Jeremiah 1:5).

The design and purpose of this chapter is to capture the new fundamental work surrounding stem cells and the potential they may provide in regards to making significant contributions to science. I recall discussing stem cells with several of my colleagues while preparing for an embryology/genetics test at Oklahoma State University College of Osteopathic Medicine in Tulsa, Oklahoma in 1989. At that time we were discovering the possible potential of stem cells although little was known about their use, how to obtain them, and more practically, how to implement them into therapeutic plans. In studying the properties that stem cells possess, it became evident how magnificent it would be to obtain these cells and use them in a disease/treatment model. Even in early stages of research we could recognize how greatly they would benefit mankind and enhance medicine's capacity. If stem cells could be obtained and grown into cell lines that would enable their use, people suffering from numerous diseases would be able to benefit from them. In my pursuit of this topic, I have come to a better appreciation for the subjects I was studying back in 1989.

I have since learned of the great dilemmas that arise out of stem cell treatment and most importantly from embryonic cell lines. There has been and will continue to be great debate about obtaining embryonic cells and their use in regards to moral, ethical, and economical issues. My purpose in writing this chapter is to discuss the basic principles of stem cells as well as the dilemmas they pose to Christians today. I firmly believe, as a physician studying stem cell research and having been in medicine for approximately twenty years, that this topic has much to offer those suffering from various acute and chronic diseases. I understand that significantly more research needs to take place to establish and perfect these treatment regimens. It is felt that millions of patients in the United States might benefit from stem cell-based therapies.

Stem Cells

In 1908, the term "stem cell" was proposed for scientific use by the Russian histologist, Alexander Maksimov (1874-1928) at the Congress of Hematological Society in Berlin. It postulated the existence of hematopoietic stem cells. There are two types of stem cells: embryonic, or unlimited stem cells, and adult stem cells, which are limited. The properties of stem cells are numerous. They are classified as multicellular organisms that have the ability to renew via mitotic divisions. They are known to differentiate into specialized cells. They possess the ability to go through several cycles of cell division while maintaining the undifferentiated state. They can be further classified in regard to their potency.

Totipotent stem cells are known to be the most potent. Totipotency is present for approximately fourteen days. Those types of cells can differentiate into embryonic and extraembryonic cells. The fertilization of an egg with a sperm has a single cell with the ability to create an entire organism. **Pluripotent** stem cells are from totipotent cells, which tend to specialize, but not create, an entire organism like the totipotent cells do. **Multipotent** stem cells also possess the ability to differentiate but only to the types that it may be closely familiar to. **Oligopotent** stem cells also are able to differentiate but are somewhat limited to only a few types of cell lines. **Unipotent** stem cells can produce essentially their own kind, which would be a single cell format. Thus, they have limited differentiation capacity.

How stem cells work can be through the processes of **plasticity** which is the potential to change into other cell types, **homing** which is the ability to travel to other sites of body tissues damaged, and **engraftment** which is the means to unite with other tissues. After stem cells are injected, they cause cytokines to be secreted, making remarkable effects occur.

Someone may ask, "What are stem cells, how do I get them, and what use would they be from a medical standpoint?" As mentioned previously, stem cells are undifferentiated cells that can be obtained from either an embryonic or an adult source. Stem cells have the ability to develop into many different cell types within the body, which could be used for repair. It is felt that these cells could continue to divide and replenish as long as the person or animal is still alive. When a stem cell divides, each "daughter" cell has the potential to either remain a stem cell or become another type of cell with a more specialized function, such as a muscle, red blood cell, or a brain cell. Additionally, stem cells have the ability to remain either undifferentiated or differentiate and contribute to the process of healing tissues. This ability is based upon their recognition and response to certain genes, proteins, antigens, and growth factors.

The development of embryonic stem cells begins with the fertilization between the egg and the sperm. Some consider this conception; however, as discussed in Chapter 1, conception carries different connotations depending on ethnic, cultural, or religious backgrounds. After fertilization, a two-cell stage forms, leading to further progression with a four-cell stage, then a morula, and then to a blastocyst. During the first four to five days of development, the blastocyte consists of fifty to 150 cells, which are pluripotent, eventually differentiating into primary germ layers: ectoderm, endoderm, and mesoderm. They then eventually develop into more than 200 cell types.

Embryonic stem cells that have been obtained carry the pluripotent ability and can be cultured and grown indefinitely in a laboratory, which can create cell culture lines. Essentially, they can be considered as immortal regardless of how they were derived. They may be frozen for storage and later distributed to other researchers. The complexity, however, lies in the engineering process of these cell lines regarding transplantation or the treatment for diseases. Problems may occur regarding rejection secondary to the patient's immune system. That is why further research is warranted. As further identified, this is why pluripotent stem cells have the greatest therapeutic potential. However, new strides are being made regarding multipotent stem cells, which may diminish the need for embryonic stem cells, therefore resolving the dilemma of destruction of embryos. It will be mandatory, however, for purified cell lines to be derived prior to their use.

Adult stem cells, on the other hand, have the potential for self-renewal, can be multipotent, and may lack differentiation until they receive the appropriate environmental signals that have led to their designation as adult stem cells, although they are sometimes designated more conservatively as progenitor cells. They are referred to as adult stem cells to distinguish them from embryonic stem cells, even if they are taken from fetal or neonatal sources. Their source of location, as well as their potential, are also responsible for part of their classification. The sources of adult stem cells are numerous including many of the organs. It has also been discovered that these stem cells possess the ability to transdifferentiate into other tissue types depending on their location in the body. This provides many opportunities for treatment of various disorders.

Adult stem cell treatment has been ongoing for several years and is not new to medicine at this time. An example of this would be the treatment currently for leukemia/blood cancers through bone marrow transplants. In the 1960's, research was done by a Canadian, Ernest McCulloch, and James E. Till and they were able to show the self-renewing cells in mouse bone marrow. However, it is now recognized that there are more populations of stem cell lines than previously expected. Hopefully, with time and scientific advances in technology, greater discovery will be obtained and more treatment options will be given.

In August of 2001 then President George W. Bush signed a bill limiting federal funding for research involving human embryonic stem cell lines created after that date. Existing cell lines were able to be used, although no new cell lines were able to be created through and paid for by federal funds. However, it had always been available for private sector funding to support embryonic stem cell research. Prior to George W. Bush's signing, in 1993, President Bill Clinton gave the NIH direct authority to fund human embryo research for the very first time. Subsequently, in 1995, the U. S. Congress passed an appropriations bill. Attached to the bill was the Dickey amendment, a rider that prohibited federally appropriated funds to be used for research where human embryos would be either created or destroyed. This predates the creation of the first human embryonic stem cell lines.

After the creation of the first human embryonic stem cell lines in 1998 by James Thomason of the University of Wisconsin, Harriott Rabb, the top lawyer of the Department of Health and Human Services released a legal opinion that would set the course for the Clinton administration policy in 1999. Federal funds, obviously, could not be used to derive stem cell lines because this involves embryo destruction. However, she concluded that because human embryonic stem cells "are not a human embryo within the statutory definition, the Dickey/Wicker amendment does not apply to them." The NIH was, therefore, free to give federal funding to experiments involving the cells themselves. President Clinton strongly endorsed the new guidelines, noting that human embryonic stem cell research promised "potentially staggering benefits." However, as dually noted, Bush's signature of the bill prevented new funding after 2001 for any created embryonic cell line.

On March 9, 2009 President Barack Obama lifted the federal restriction for funding of embryonic stem cell research bringing the debate full circle. Mr. Obama stated, "We will vigorously support scientist who pursue this research and we will aim for America to lead the world in the discoveries it one day may yield." President Obama further stated, "As a person of faith, I believe we are called to care for each other and work to ease human suffering. I believe we have been given the capacity and will to pursue this research and the humanity and conscience to do so responsibly."

There are several questions to be addressed regarding the use of stem cells. First, is cell replacement therapy safe and effective in human beings? Secondly, is it ethical to use embryonic cells for research in therapies? Finally, is it ethical to use adult stem cells in research? As previously mentioned, there are millions of patients in the United States who could potentially benefit from stem cell therapy. Most would not argue against adult stem cell research, the dilemma is how to treat embryonic stem cells. As already noted, recipients have been saved due to the efforts from those who have developed adult stem cell therapies. Potential therapeutic uses of stem cells range from a variety of diseases including Parkinson's, osteoporosis, autoimmune, cardiovascular, Alzheimer's, diabetes, spinal cord injuries, ophthalmological processes such as retinal degeneration, macular degeneration, brain tumors, metabolic diseases, hematological diseases and cancers. Theoretically the list could go on. Understand that it will take time and money to further the process. That is why additional research is warranted to support the safety and efficacy questions.

Recently, we have seen the push by Michael J. Fox for the support of stem cell research for Parkinson's disease, which he suffers from. Also, we have seen the struggles that Christopher Reeves endured from his spinal cord injury, which subsequently took his life due to secondary complications. It was his desire as well as Michael J. Fox's that research in this field continues so some day cures and treatments for their respective problems can be found.

It is felt that human embryonic stem cells have a much greater developmental potential than the adult stem cells that have been discussed. Why then such controversy? Simply put, the controversy arises from embryonic stem cells being derived from an embryo that has been destroyed. The federal policy signed by George W. Bush in 2001 stated that no embryo should be created for the destruction of its use. There are many who oppose embryonic stem cell research based on their ethnic, cultural, or religious views. Yes, we all came from embryos; however, there are various definitions of what describes an embryo, which creates further controversy. Some will use the term "pre embryo," which is from the zygote phase, which is the union of a sperm and an egg until approximately fourteen days. This phase is prior to the primitive streak that will develop. From two to approximately seven or eight weeks it is then classified as an embryo. Beyond the seventh or eighth week, the classification is a fetus until delivery. Also, to give further controversy to the debate of embryonic stem cell use is the term "conception" as discussed in Chapter 1. In the same way, everybody admits that the human sperm and egg are not human beings, but jointly have the potential to become a human being, given fertilization, time, development, and the right conditions. We all agree that we derive from an embryo state. We also all agree that an embryo, regardless of the definition, must have been implanted and attached to the uterine wall to begin its developmental path towards personhood. When fertilization occurs *in vitro*, outside the body, the fertilized egg is not deprived of any future life if it is not implanted. A fertilized embryo *in vitro* is not on its way toward a future life; left by itself it will inevitably die. Not implanting an embryo fertilized *in vitro* does not cause it to lose future life that it otherwise would have had, rather it simply omits its potential future life that the embryo otherwise would not have had.

We know already that there are numerous spare embryos in existence in laboratories that will never be implanted. There are many who disagree with the research of embryonic stem cells because it is unethical to destroy the blastocyst, which is an unimplanted human embryo at the sixth to eighth day of development. Some view this as the taking of innocent human life. Proponents for research argue, however, that a blastocyst is simply a cluster of cells that may be anywhere from fifty to 200 cells growing in a petri dish. They do not have the characteristics of human form or features. It is not recognizable in any shape, form or fashion, thus they have not differentiated. This is precisely the reason that proponents want to use them.

Senator Sam Brownback, Republican of Kansas, advocates that a human embryo is a human being just like you and me and deserves the same respect that our laws give to us all. If he is correct, then embryonic stem cell research is immoral because it amounts to killing a person to treat other people's diseases. But is he right? Many disagree with this reasoning, stating that any living human cell (a skin cell, for example) is "human life." "Human life" in this instance would be defined as human rather than bovine and living rather than dead, but no one would consider a skin cell a person or deem it inviolable. Showing that a blastocyst is a human being, or a person, requires further argument. Opponents for embryonic stem cell research argue that an embryo as a person, fully respected of all moral and ethical obligations, is not persuasive enough because that embryo has not achieved personhood and is, therefore, not the taking of innocent life. I have heard this analogy described like this: Although every oak tree was once an acorn, it does not follow that acorns are oak trees or that I should treat the loss of an acorn eaten by a squirrel in my front yard as the same kind of loss as the death of an oak tree felled by a storm. Despite their development's continuity, acorns and oak trees differ. Human embryos and human beings differ in the same way. Just as acorns are potential oaks, human embryos are potential human beings. The claim is that the distinction between a potential person and an actual person makes a moral difference. If persuaded that embryonic stem cell research is parallel to infanticide, then not only would we ban it, but we would treat it as a grizzly form of murder and subject scientists who perform it to criminal punishment. However, this is not the case as there are many fertility clinics in this country presently with petri dishes consisting of zygotes. The question is: What happens to those that are left over after successful implantation has been carried out? If discarded, then this is in essence the same as killing children if the belief is that they are human beings. Therefore, the question of defining personhood is essential as discussed in Chapter 2. Even more so is the topic of ensoulment. That is a question that obviously will never be answered. While it is known that each cell is alive, it is also known that they only become part of a human organism when there is substantial cell differentiation and coordination, which occurs around days

14-16 after fertilization. Thus, removing cells prior to this date would not be destroying a human being. These cells outside of the right environment, i.e. uterus, will never develop into a mature human being.

Some have viewed using embryonic stem cell research similar to donating bodies to science or donating organs for the purpose of research or to help others who are in need, the same as donating an egg or sperm to research. Some feel that, since embryonic cells taken from the blastocyst carry no human form, have no nervous system, are not persons or human beings, and have no soul, therefore the embryonic cell does not have the protection entitled to persons or human beings. Ensoulment as well as establishment of personhood also make the challenge regarding moral status when debating the topic of embryonic stem cell research complex.

In further discussion of the forming embryo, many scientists assign significant importance to the primitive streak. As we have noted, before the primitive streak, the cells are essentially undifferentiated. The primitive streak is the stage of development that leads to the embryological growth ultimately leading to a biological identity. Many feel that this is the stage when one is considered a human individual and personhood is achieved. There are so many processes ongoing during this critical period responsible for this new creation. It is at this point when organs and structures will be designated and be committed for further growth. It is fascinating how this development occurs in such a short time. The circulatory system is believed to be the first to form. This dynamic development will eventually be responsible for the vital nutritional requirements needed for the many organs and structures to follow. There are several arguments being made against the practice of embryonic research basically because the premise of destroying the "embryo" and subsequently not allowing it to undergo its natural progression. This embryonic development is what would occur during *in vivo,* i.e. the womb. It is outside the womb in fertility clinics where frozen "embryos" are contained that gives rise to the big controversial issue regarding "left over embryos." What is to be done with the embryos when the donor no longer wishes to have them implanted, offers them to a surrogate recipient or denies them to be discarded? Is it ethical to use them in stem cell research? Many would say no. There are various biblical Scriptures used to denounce any research on embryonic stem cells, one being Psalm 139:16 which reads, "Thine eyes have seen my unformed substance" and another Psalm 127:3 reading, "Behold children are a gift of the Lord, the fruit of the womb is a reward." However, I feel these verses are difficult to apply in regards to the circumstances given. These cells are outside their normal environment and will not develop further unless *in vitro* implantation occurs. Another passage cited against embryonic stem cell research is Jeremiah 1:5, "Before I formed you in the womb I knew you, and before you were born I consecrated you." This is speaking directly to Jeremiah. This passage of itself would not preclude embryonic stem cell research. Once again, what is to happen to those "left over embryos"? I do not know, but some of the greatest challenges that lie ahead in medicine can be dealt with through research done by embryonic stem cells. There are still many questions to ask regarding this topic and further investigation is necessary to find the answers. Genesis 2:7 states, "Then the Lord God formed man of dust from the ground, and breathed into his nostrils the breath of life; and man became a living being" – a passage that has relevance to every human. I thank God for every day He has given me. I am gracious for His rich blessings and take nothing for granted.

As a physician, it is my obligation to provide my patients with the best treatment that is reasonable, safe, and effective as well as ethical (i.e., not violating God's word). I am more than willing to serve them with these constraints in mind. Throughout my years, I have seen great advancements and strides in medicine that are staggering. With the aid of new diagnostic tools, the push for advanced medications, and the discovery of new therapies, we are able to provide a better quality of care to those who are in need. We don't have all the answers that stem cells have to offer. With the new recent developments regarding adult stem cells, there arises the potential that embryonic stem cells may not be necessary and, therefore, eliminates the dilemmas or debates about their use. President Barack Obama has reversed the ban on future embryonic stem cell research. We are seeing the literature discussions about stem cells and their potential uses every day. This we do know; that man has benefited from stem cell research and will continue to do so. However, I give caution to when it comes to creating stem cell farms just for the sake of research. It will be a slippery slope for those who want to donate only for the monetary value. My position is in regards to the "left over embryos." The question is: how many more people can we help? The controversies and debates will continue. Stem cell research or its uses transcend any political affiliation or economic status you may obtain. You need to make your own decision where you stand on this topic.

Chapter 5
Birth Control and Artificial Fertilization

Behold, children are a gift of the Lord, the fruit of the womb is a reward (Psalm 127:3).

In this chapter, we will examine the issue of birth control and artificial fertilization. We will look at various methods used currently to prevent and achieve pregnancy and attempt to determine if any or all violate Christian ethics. Before doing this, we should first ask the question "Is it right for Christians to practice any form of birth control?"

Some have argued that children are a gift of God and nothing should be done in marriage to prohibit the natural consequences of the sexual relationship that eventually results in pregnancy. Those holding such positions refer to Psalms 127:3-5. This passage reads: "Behold children are a gift of the Lord; the fruit of the womb is a reward. Like arrows in the hand of a warrior, so are the children of one's youth. How blessed is the man whose quiver is full of them, they shall not be ashamed, when they speak with their enemies in the gate."

Clearly, children are indeed a blessing from God and should be cherished and raised in the admonition of the Lord (Ephesians 6:4). There is, however, nothing in Psalms 127 to infer that birth control is prohibited by God. In 1 Timothy 5:8, Paul writes "But if anyone does not provide for his own, and especially for those of his household, he hath denied the faith, and is worse than an unbeliever." Families with too many children who cannot adequately care for them are in violation of this scripture.

There is at least one incident in the Bible that condemns a form of birth control known as "coitus interruptus." This occurs in Genesis 38 where Onan, the brother of the deceased Er, was instructed to "go into" Tamar to perform his duty so she would conceive and raise up children in the name of Er. Onan knew the children would not be his, according to verse 9, and, therefore, "wasted his seed on the ground," thereby preventing conception by Tamar. This displeased God who took Onan's life as result. In this case, "birth control" was condemned by God but, in the context, the reason is apparent. Onan was not fulfilling his brotherly duty according to law to raise up children in Er's name. It would be a stretch to prohibit birth control based upon this one incident in the Bible. This was condemned for a specific reason and, therefore, it should not be generalized. There is no other biblical passage we are aware of that specifically or generally condemns the practice of birth control. There is at least one passage that at least infers that one "method" of birth control is acceptable and this is found in 1 Corinthians 7:5. Here, Paul writes to the married, "Stop depriving one another except by agreement for a time, that you may devote yourself to prayer, and come together again lest Satan tempt you because of your lack of self control." The birth control method here is abstinence. Admittedly, this scripture is not dealing specifically with birth control but clearly abstinence would prohibit pregnancy from occurring.

The Catholic Church position, save for the rhythm method, holds that contraception is wrong because it is a deliberate violation of the design built into the human race by God in the form of natural law. They believe the natural law purpose for sex is procreation and pleasure during sexual intercourse is simply an additional blessing from God. The "Church" teaches sexual pleasure within marriage becomes unnatural and may be even harmful when it deliberately excludes the basic purpose of sex, which is procreation. For example, they believe the above mentioned incidence of Onan's death in Genesis 38 was for practicing contraception and, once a moral principle is stated in the Bible, it becomes established and its application need not be mentioned elsewhere. The Catholic Church also points to "church fathers" such as Clement of Alexandria, Hippolytus of Rome, and Lactantius, who condemned the practice of contraception. Further stated on the Catholic web site, "Catholic Answers," Protestant reformers, such as John Calvin and John Wesley, taught against birth control. They even go so far as to equate contraception with "free love" and infidelity and allude to a "recent study" that revealed divorce rates in marriages are greater when contraception is regularly practiced. On the same website, they maintain the Church "has always taught that deliberate acts of contraception are always gravely sinful, which means that it is morally sinful if done with full knowledge and deliberate consent."

Unfortunately, the Catholic Church ignores biblical teaching. Genesis 2:18, states that God created woman as a "helper" suitable for him (Adam). Paul, through the Holy Spirit, writes in 1 Corinthians 7 that the sexual relationship between man and woman is clearly not just for the purpose of procreation.

The question then is, "Are all forms of birth control ethical from a Christian perspective?" The answer may depend on what type of birth control we are talking about. For birth control to be morally right, it should not violate the biblical principle of the shedding of innocent blood. We believe abortion certainly fits this prohibition and unfortunately, as we discussed in the Preface of this book, many use abortion as a type of birth control. We believe birth control practices that do not violate the shedding of innocent blood principle are permissible by God. It is time now to examine these practices and see how they work to determine their ethics.

Methods of Birth Control

Current birth control methods range from abstinence to birth control pills. Broadly speaking, birth control either prevents fertilization or it prevents implantation unless we are talking about an abortifacient, which causes loss of implanted embryos. Let's look at those methods that prevent fertilization first. Clearly, any method that prevents sperm from getting to the ovum prevents fertilization, hence pregnancy. Coitus interruptus is one such method as determined earlier in the case of Onan in the book of Genesis. In this method, the male withdraws from the female before ejaculation. This method is not 100% effective since some sperm are released before ejaculation occurs. The so-called rhythm method is also used for the prevention of pregnancy. This involves the deliberate refraining from sexual intercourse during times when pregnancy is most likely; that is, when ovulation occurs which is the tenth to fourteenth day of a woman's cycle. The failure rate of periodic abstinence, however, is 20%, and requires frequent monitoring of body functions. Barrier methods also prevent pregnancy clearly by not allowing the sperm to reach the ovum. These methods include male and female condoms as well as the diaphragm. The Lea's shield on the cervical cap with spermicide, as well as the sponge with spermicide are also barrier methods but include chemicals that affect sperm mobility and viability. One way in which the IUD works is to also prevent sperm from entering the fallopian tube, thereby preventing pregnancy. Spermicide gels work by "killing the sperm." Finally, surgical sterilization in the female in the form of tubaligation and in the male in the form of a vasectomy also work as "barrier methods" in preventing either sperm from entering the fallopian tube or at least not the portion of the tube where fertilization occurs. The efficacy and the side effects of these methods can all be found in the Birth Control Guide published by the FDA and available on their web site. Briefly, though, with the exception of the IUD, barrier methods are considered safe and variously effective; the least effective being spermicidal gels alone and the most effective being surgical sterilization with a pregnancy rate of less than 1%. The IUD, however, has been problematic in some cases, its primary side effect being pelvic inflammatory disease and even perforation of the uterus, which has potentially very serious consequences. Once widely used, IUD's have fallen out of favor, although there seems to be a bit of resurgence in their use of late.

Very commonly used birth control methods today involve hormonal treatment, either in the form of birth control pills or an injectable progesterone and estrogen. Birth control pills gained significant popularity in the 1960's and remain very popular today. They are very effective in preventing pregnancy with only a 1 to 2% failure rate and no doubt were at least partly responsible for the sexual revolution seen in the 1960's in this country. There are many types of birth control pills and hormonal injections that differ in the percentages of progestin or estrogen. Basically, they all work primarily in the prevention of ovulation through the interaction in the pituitary gland. Obviously, if there is no ovum in the fallopian tube at the time of intercourse, fertilization will not take place. There are some cases, however, of "escape ovulation" explaining at least in part the 1 to 2% failure rate seen in these methods. Some have argued that birth control pills are also abortifacients since they also may change uterine mucosa, thereby inhibiting implantation. There is also some evidence of changes in the cervical secretions that may inhibit both sperm mobility as well as possible implantation but no scientific research we are aware of demonstrates birth control pills to be abortifacients as obviously women do become pregnant while on the birth control pill when "escape ovulation" occurs. In our previous chapter, we pointed out spontaneous abortions or miscarriages occur anywhere from 20% to 50% of the time. When one factors in this data with the phenomenon of "escape ovulation" that occurs with birth control pills, it appears extremely doubtful that birth control pills prevent implantation as one of their modes of action.

This is an important point. Opponents of all hormonal contraceptives have made the argument that birth control pills statistically increase ectopic pregnancy rates. In doing so, however, they combine both combined oral contraceptives that is progesterone and estrogen contraceptives, with progesterone-only pills to arrive at their conclusions. If progesterone-only pills are excluded there appears to be no increased incidents in ectopic pregnancies with combined oral contraceptives. Dr. Dennis Sullivan, in his article, "The Oral Contraceptive as Abortifacient: An Analysis of the Evidence," states, "To summarize the scientific case indicting combined oral contraceptives as having an abortifacient action, the evidence appears inconclusive at the present time. With present medical understanding, the issue cannot be completely resolved." The problem is in identifying precisely when breakthrough ovulation occurs during combined oral contraceptive use and when fertilization occurs. Current standard pregnancy tests using HCG in maternal blood do not rise to a measurable quantity until after implantation. There is, however, a maternal protein called "early pregnancy factor" (EPF) that can measure fertilization before implantation. Used only as a research tool at present, EPF could be valuable in discriminating between failure to fertilize and failure to implant. Using this knowledge, further research on EPF as a diagnostic tool may help to determine if combined oral contraceptives are in fact abortifacient. At this time, we know of no ongoing studies to determine this; however, it should be reiterated, the mechanism of the combined oral contraceptives is the prevention of ovulation.

Birth control pills and progesterone/estrogen injections do have potential serious side effects, however. The major concern with estrogen/progesterone birth control pills is the increased risk of blood clots that can cause strokes, heart attacks, and pulmonary embolisms, all with potential life-threatening consequences. These risks of serious side effects go up with age and increase in cigarette smokers. Progesterone-only oral contraceptives also have as side effects, irregular bleeding, weight gain, breast tenderness, and less protection against ectopic pregnancy. Depo-Provera injections, that is, progesterone-only injections inhibit ovulation, prevent sperm from reaching the egg, and prevent fertilized eggs from implanting in the uterus. Irregular bleeding, weight gain, breast tenderness, and headaches are their major side effects. Finally, implant devices that release contraceptive steroid continuously, the most notable being Norplant, introduced in the 1990's, works similarly to the birth control pill with similar effective birth control rates and again with similar side effects, although cardiovascular risks are not as prevalent. The choice of using birth control pills then becomes an individual decision. We do not believe they prohibit biblical principles, as they do not result in the shedding of innocent blood.

We would like to look briefly at two other methods of birth control before leaving this topic. First, the "morning-after pill" was approved by the FDA in 1998 and 1999. The morning-after pill contains either progestin alone or progesterone plus estrogen with trade names being Prevn and Plan B. Clearly, as their names imply, a woman takes these pills after coitus and must be taken within seventy-two hours after unprotected intercourse to be effective. They are approximately 80% effective in reducing the risk of pregnancy from a single act of unprotected sex. Many believe the morning-after pill to be an abortifacient. This, however, is not the case. As discussed in Chapter 2, implantation does not occur until the tenth day or later after fertilization; thus for a pill taken the morning after intercourse, the "aborting" of a pregnancy could not occur because the morning after is much too early for implantation. The fact is the morning-after pills work primarily like birth control pills by preventing ovulation. A woman might be ovulating on the night of intercourse and the primary effect of the morning after pill is to prevent this ovulation and thus fertilization. Admittedly, the morning-after pill probably does change uterine mucosa and thereby could also work in preventing implantation and thus serve as a further hindrance to pregnancy. Because of this, Christian women may very well be better served using some other form of birth control. The question here arises as to why a Christian would choose this method to begin with. The morning-after pill is primarily used for "unexpected intercourse" and this usually occurs in a non-marriage situation. In this case, the morning-after pill is used when fornication is being practiced which is clearly condemned by God.

Sometimes confused with the morning-after pill is the abortion pill known as RU-486. Introduced in 2000 and approved by the FDA, the RU-486 pill is taken within forty-nine days, that is, within seven weeks after the start of the last menstrual period, when pregnancy has occurred. It is an "anti-progestin." This triggers the shedding of uterine wall much like a normal period, thus causing the expulsion of the developing embryo. One or two days after taking the RU-486 pill, the woman takes a prostaglandin pill, typically Misoprostol. This causes the cervix to soften and dilate, contractions of the uterus to occur, and the embryo is expelled within four hours in 54% of the cases and within twenty-four hours in 22% of the cases. The "success" rate of this type of chemical abortion is in the 99% range. Some, up to 2-3%, will experience incomplete abortion, requiring surgical abortion. Rarely, excessive bleeding can occur and other side effects include significant cramping, nausea, and other milder systemic side effects. It is our belief the RU-486 pill violates the biblical principle of the shedding of innocent blood and, therefore, should not be used as a birth control method.

In summary, there are many birth control methods currently available for use. Christian couples should determine what suits their particular situation best and choose those methods that are safest and clearly those that do not involve the shedding of innocent blood, which is in violation of God's principles. As mentioned earlier, a guide to birth control practices is published by various organizations including the FDA of the United States Government and are available on various web sites. Please note the authors do not condone or advise necessarily any particular methods that appear on these sites.

Artificial Fertilization

The antithesis of birth control is artificial fertilization, primarily by way of *in vivo* or *in vitro* fertilization. *In vivo* fertilization is the fertilization of an ovum within the distal fallopian tube of a fertile donor female rather than an artificial medium by subsequent, nonsurgical transfer to an infertile recipient. For practical purposes and for reasons to be discussed later, *in vivo* fertilization is rarely used today. More commonly, *in vitro* fertilization has been used since the last 1970's in couples who, for other reasons, are unable to achieve pregnancy through natural means. This occurs when there is tubal sterility in the female, either by obstruction secondary to scar tissue from infections, genetically obstructed fallopian tubes, or even voluntary sterilization through tubal ligation. *In vitro* fertilization, however, is also used due to male subfertilities such as a decrease in the number of competent spermatozoa, immobile spermatozoa, or even in cases of surgical sterility in a male through vasectomy. Sometimes *in vitro* fertilization is used when there are other inexplicable reasons for infertility. *In vitro* fertilization is now common with over 360 fertilization clinics throughout the United States.

The process of *in vitro* fertilization first begins with the woman taking follicle-stimulating hormones in order to produce multiple ovulations. This is done in order to harvest as many ovum as possible as frequently *in vitro* fertilizations are unsuccessful. With multiple eggs harvested, more attempts can be tried later. The woman usually also takes drugs containing HCG to stimulate further maturation of the eggs. After ovulation or just before ovulation, eggs are retrieved from a woman's ovaries, usually using a needle through ultrasound guidance, although they can also be retrieved laproscopically. The eggs are then transferred to a laboratory dish with specially prepared medium where they are then combined with sperm for fertilization. Before fertilization takes placed, eggs are examined to determine the healthiest ones. At this point, natural results are allowed to happen with the hope that several eggs will be fertilized. In the case of severe male infertility, a single egg will be injected with a single sperm called "intra-cytoplasmic sperm injection" or ICSI. Because only one sperm is needed, ICSI can offer fertilization in couples where sperm would otherwise not impregnate the ovum. Once multiple fertilized eggs have been obtained, they can now be tested for pre-implantation genetic diseases (PGD) such as cystic fibrosis and Tay-Sachs disease. In fact there are now at least 92 single gene disorders that can be tested for before implantation if parents so desire, with the field of PGD rapidly expanding. Though currently used in testing for disease, in the future a pre-implantation test will include examining for non-disease "traits" such as hair color, eye color, height, intelligence, athletic potential, and a host of other characteristics. In the future it may be possible to "treat" or enhance pre-implanted embryos with genetic therapies and other modalities.

Once appropriate eggs are selected, they are then transferred into the woman's uterus or possibly into a surrogate uterus, where embryonic development is anticipated. Usually, two or more fertilized eggs are transferred because spontaneous miscarriage occurs frequently with *in vitro* fertilization. If more than one embryo develops *in utero*, the other viable embryos can be removed for the option of cryopreserving. This decreases the risk of multiple gestations; twins, triplets, quadruplets, etc., from occurring *in utero*. These developing embryos can be preserved, usually for up to a term of five years, at which time the couple then must decide to either donate to science, donate to another couple, or have those embryos destroyed. The overall success rate for *in vitro* fertilization is approximately 20% and costs from $12,000 to $14,000. The success rate of *in vitro* fertilizations significantly decreases with the increasing age of the woman.

Several ethical dilemmas are encountered with *in vitro* fertilization. For example, what is done with the fertilized eggs that are not transferred *in utero*? Furthermore, what happens to the removed embryos after five years of cryopreservation? According to a survey of 239 *in vitro* fertilization clinics taken in 1998, excess "embryos" are (1) immediately discarded (49.6%), (2) allowed to expire on their own (46.1%), (3) donated to research (23.7%), (4) donated to create diagnostic test (11.6%), (5) donated to train fertility clinic staff (22.4%), (6) or donated to another couple or "patient" (18.5%). (NOTE: Percentages exceed 100% because many clinics exercise more than one option.) Few rules dictate what happens to the "embryos" that are not implanted as long as patient consent is given, notwithstanding President George W. Bush's ban on embryonic stem cell research. Presently, there are no absolute numbers of fertilized eggs in storage but it is estimated there are over 200,000 in over 360 in vitro clinics throughout the United States. Another important question from a legal standpoint is: Who do these eggs now belong to, the man or the woman? When divorce occurs, this becomes a very big issue and court cases are pending trying to answer these questions. Also, who has the right to destroy, transfer, or otherwise dispose of fertilized eggs or embryos that have occurred during this *in vitro* fertilization. These are significant questions Christian couples should entertain when considering *in vitro* fertilization. Certainly, fertilized eggs, as discussed in Chapter 1, do not meet the definition of personhood, but clearly potential for personhood exists. A further question to be entertained is: Why is *in vitro* fertilization being contemplated? Is *in vitro* just a form of vanity? Maybe in some cases, adoption is the best answer for couples desirous of raising a family. Obviously, it becomes a matter of judgment within each individual situation.

Pre-implantation testing also raises several ethical questions. For one, it is a form of eugenics involving the practice of improving the human gene pool by eliminating undesired embryos. Yet, what parent would not want to select the "best" embryo for implantation? Furthermore, in the future will only the wealthy be able to afford genetic enhancement therapies, thereby propagating an elite upper class? Also could this lead to discrimination of those already disabled? Another ethical concern and currently being practiced is the use of pre-implantation diagnosis to select for siblings whose blood types and genotypes will be compatible for treating sick older siblings. Currently this is being done when an older sibling is born with a congenital disease requiring bone marrow transplantation. Parents are purposely selecting fertilized embryos in order to obtain compatible bone marrow. Is this moral or ethical? Many other ethical questions can be imagined and in the future it may become necessary for some limitations to be placed on pre-implantation diagnosis, selection, and treatments, yet all reproduction clinics currently apply at least some means of selecting the "best" fertilized eggs for implantation. Medical science may not have yet "designed" a baby but some "designing" is achieved when a medical procedure is done at pre-implantation to avoid a congenital disease.

Sexuality and Sexually Transmitted Disease

Before leaving the subject of birth control and artificial fertilization, it seems expedient to say a few words about sexuality and sexually transmitted diseases. The Bible is very clear; God has never condoned sex between non-married individuals. The sexual union between man and woman since the beginning of time with Adam and Eve is always to be between a husband and wife. When sex occurs between non-married couples, it is always condemned in the Old and New Testament. Having said that, the sexual relationship between a man and woman is a gift of God and to be considered a divine blessing. Hebrew 13:4 says, "Let marriage be held in honor among all, and let the marriage bed be undefiled; for fornicators and adulterers God will judge." Those who believe marriage is simply for the purpose of procreation fail to understand God's word as evidenced by the previous verse. Paul also alludes to the importance of the sexual bond between husband and wife in 1 Corinthians 7:1-9. Paul instructs husbands and wives to fulfill their duties to one another and to "stop depriving one another except by agreement for a time that you may devote yourselves to prayer and come together again, lest Satan tempts you because of your lack of self control." It should be understood that God ordains marriage but marriage ceremonies differ between cultures and societies and the ceremony itself is immaterial. When marriage occurs between a man and woman, it is God that binds that marriage and it is not for man to break that bond according to Matthew 19:6. In this verse, Jesus is answering questions posed by the Pharisees concerning the lawfulness of divorce. Jesus points out because of the hardness of their hearts, Moses permitted divorce, but from the beginning "it has not been this way." Christ further states in verse 9, "Whoever divorces his wife, except for immorality, and marries another woman, commits adultery." The importance of the sexual union between a man and woman can be seen in this verse, as it is the only cause for divorce given by our Lord. Clearly, it is incumbent that men and women, boys and girls, understand this important relationship before entering into marriage and before engaging in sexual activities outside the marriage bond, clearly prohibited by God. It is very, very important to honor the sanctity of marriage and when those vows are broken, as sometimes occurs, it is very difficult to heal that relationship. Untold numbers of marriages have been ruined, destroyed, or irreversibly damaged by the infidelity of one or the other spouse.

With these thoughts understood, we will look briefly at sexually transmitted diseases. In a perfect world, sexually transmitted diseases would completely disappear if man would obey God's commandment concerning sex and marriage. Unfortunately, man does not obey God's word and the prevalence of sexually transmitted diseases is epidemic throughout the world with an estimated 1 in 3 men or women contacting a sexual disease sometime in their life. Although many sexually transmitted diseases can be adequately treated, with the advent of the human immunovirus (HIV) many millions have died, and millions are still afflicted by this disease, which is primarily transmitted through sexual intercourse. Other sexually transmitted diseases include chlamydia, syphilis, gonorrhea, trichomonas, herpes simplex type II virus, and even hepatitis B and C. Sexually pure couples, that is, those who remain non-sexual before marriage and faithful to one another after marriage, never have to worry about most of these disorders, save for those transmitted through blood transfusions and the sharing of intimate objects such as razors and needles. Even the human papilloma virus (HPV), responsible for cervical cancer, is transmitted sexually and could be avoided.

Teenage pregnancies and unwanted adult pregnancies between non-married couples obviously would cease if God's words were obeyed. Unfortunately, once again, this is not the case and many unwanted pregnancies result in early termination by abortion. The ethical or moral question is: Should our children be educated about sexually transmitted diseases and human sexuality in public schools? It is our belief these subjects should best be discussed between the parents of young boys and girls. All too often this responsibility is delegated to our public school system and as a result, instead of teaching abstinence or "Just Say No," our children are taught about "safe sex" and the use of condoms to prevent pregnancy and sexually transmitted diseases. Clearly, from the number of sexually transmitted diseases and unwanted teenage pregnancies occurring in our country, we are not doing an adequate job. One group attempting to rectify this problem is the "Worth the Wait" program from the Scott and White Clinic in Texas. This medical based program offers educational materials to churches, public and private schools, and other interested parties. This program emphasizes the importance of delaying sexual activity until after marriage.

Parents need to talk to their children regarding responsibilities of marriage and the importance of remaining sexually pure before marriage. They need to know marriage is not just for the sake of raising children but also involves the sexual gratification that occurs between man and wife. They further need to know, as alluded to earlier, the marriage bond is meant to be for life. Only the death of one or the other spouse should terminate the marriage, save for the exception of infidelity, mentioned in Matthew 19. These are vitally important topics to discuss with our children.

Finally, another ethical question to consider is: Can a Christian or, indeed, should a Christian use protective maneuvers in avoiding sexually transmitted diseases? Specifically, a new vaccine commercially known as Gardasil has been introduced to help protect woman from contracting the HPV virus responsible for cervical cancer. In fact, in Texas, in 2007, Governor Rick Perry introduced regulation requiring the administration of Gardasil vaccine to all teenage girls in public schools although this was later overturned. As stated earlier, if a man and woman remain sexually pure before marriage and after marriage, sexually transmitted diseases would not and could not occur. Unfortunately, this is not always the case and in our society is not even likely the case. If one partner has remained sexually pure before marriage but the other has not, then the innocent party has potential exposure to sexually transmitted diseases the other partner may have contracted. For this reason, it seems advisable for a Christian girl to consider the Guardasil vaccine. In reality, we have been vaccinating against STDs for a long time when one considers that hepatitis B can be transmitted sexually. Currently, other vaccines are being developed including those for HIV. If they become available, using the above reasoning, it would seem prudent for Christian boys and girls to take advantage of. Having said this, clearly, this should be a decision made between a young man or a young woman and their parents and should not be mandated by government organizations.

Chapter 6
Sexual Ambiguity and Chromosomal Abnormalities

And God created man in His own image, in the image of God he created him; male and female He created them (Genesis 1:27).

Chromosomal abnormalities, some of which result in sexual ambiguity, occur sometimes. They are always an anomaly and result in a less than a perfect organism. When these occur in humans, they result in children that have sexual characteristics that can be problematic and not always evident. It is not in the scope of this book to cover all the syndromes caused by chromosomal abnormalities or even to discuss all those that result in sexual ambiguity or dysfunction. We will, however, look at some of these disorders with special attention paid to those that result in true sexual ambiguity, which fortunately are exceedingly rare. At this point, one might ask: Why does God allow chromosomal abnormalities to happen? This can only be answered by asking a similar question, how did any disease enter the earth? Christians understand that by a man, Adam, sin entered into a perfect world and as a result, mankind was doomed to die. As a result, man and woman were removed from the garden and disease entered the earth with all men subject to death. Romans 5:12, says, "Therefore, just as through one man sin entered into the world, and death through sin, and so death spread to all men because all sinned." Hebrew 9:27, furthermore states, "It is appointed for man to die once and after this the judgment." These passages do not mean that all mankind inherit the sins of Adam or Eve, but rather all humankind inherited the consequence of their sins. Nonetheless, the Bible does say, "All have sinned and fallen short of the Glory of God" (Romans 3:23).

As a result, we all have imperfect bodies and we all die. This is not to say a person born with a chromosomal defect has been born this way because of sin he has committed or, for that matter, that his mother or father has committed. These individuals are simply the happenstances of life with no more explanation than that. Fortunately, with modern medical treatment, most, if not all, of these disorders can be treated.

One might also ask why this discussion belongs in a book dealing with Christian Ethics. Some of these disorders, as we shall see, do present some dilemmas, especially as it regards their treatment and the determination of sexual orientation. Exactly how one decides these questions will involve issues of a moral and ethical nature.

Chromosomal abnormalities that result in sexual ambiguity can be broadly placed into two categories, including disorders that occur at meiosis, resulting in an abnormal number of sex chromosomes, and disorders that are hormonal abnormalities not necessarily caused by abnormalities in the sex chromosomes. In literature the term "intersexuality" is frequently used to describe these disorders but this is not a derogatory term and refers to the individuals whose sex chromosomes, genitalia, and/or sexual characteristics are determined to be neither male nor female. When applied to the human body, the incidences of such disorders are rare, occurring in 0.018% of the population. It should be emphasized that these conditions do not result in homosexuality. Whether homosexuality is genetic will be discussed at the end of this chapter.

We will first look at "intersexuality," which results in problems occurring during meiosis. As discussed in Chapter 2 of this book, during normal fertilization, each parent supplies half the genetic material that makes up the developing individual. The female supplies one X chromosome and the male supplies either an X chromosome or a Y chromosome. This will then determine the sex of the new individual, XX – a girl, XY – a boy.

Unfortunately, problems can occur at the meiotic stage, which is the process when either the ovary or the testicle produces the egg or sperm that can result in an abnormal number of sex chromosomes. As a result of these abnormalities, conditions can occur that result in sexual ambiguity though most of the abnormal sexual chromosomal disorders clearly result in either male or female individuals. For example, if no X or Y chromosome is supplied by the male, the individual will have an XO genotype. This is known as Turner Syndrome.

Before discussing each individual sex chromosome disorder, a brief discussion of mosaicism is in order. Mosaicism occurs when not all the cells of the organism or individual have the same genotype. In other words, in the case of Turner Syndrome, some cells may express an XX genotype and others an XO genotype and so forth. As a result, there will be varying expressions of the different syndromes that will be discussed. Where there is no mosaicism, the full expression of the disorder will be seen. Where mosaicism exists, there will be varying degrees of expression. With that in mind, let's look at those disorders and the numbers of sexual chromosomes.

One of the most common disorders is Turner Syndrome. As mentioned earlier, Turner Syndrome occurs as a result of problems during in the meiotic stage of development. Individuals with Turner Syndrome will have only one X chromosome. This occurs in approximately one out of 2,000 females born. In some cases, Turner Syndrome will occur when one X chromosome is present or missing part of the other X chromosome. Because of this and mosaicism, the expression of Turner Syndrome will vary greatly. The most common feature of Turner Syndrome is short stature, the average height being four feet, eight inches, if growth hormone is not used for treatment. Most women with full expression of Turner Syndrome (90%) will experience early ovarian failure. Some will have delayed development of sexual characteristics. Here again, treatment with hormone replacement therapy using estrogen can correct much of these hormonal problems. Other characteristics may include webbing of the neck, a receding lower jaw, lower set ears, low hairline, broad chest, and other somatic characteristics. Intelligence seems to be unaffected by Turner Syndrome, though some may have difficulty with spatial/temporal processing and non-verbal memory attention. Children with Turner Syndrome, which is diagnosed by karyotyping, should be screened for heart, kidney, thyroid, and ear abnormalities, as these abnormalities are more prevalent in such individuals. Women with Turner Syndrome, as mentioned, have primary ovarian failure; however, hormonal treatment can and will cause pubertal development and menstrual periods. Otherwise, reproductive organs are normal and such individuals are capable of normal sexual relationships.

Klinefelter's syndrome is a condition caused by a chromosome aneuploidy, which results in an extra X chromosome. As a result, these individuals have XXY sex chromosomes, thus 47 total chromosomes as opposed to the normal of 46. The results usually cause small testicles and reduced fertility. There are a wide variety of behavioral and physical problems that can occur but again expression can be significantly varied. In non-mosaics, almost all are effectively sterile. The word "hypogonadism," sometimes used to describe Klinefelter's Syndrome, can result in decreased testicular hormones and endocrine function. Such individuals are at increased risk for certain germ cell tumors, breast cancer, and osteoporosis. Possible somatic characteristics can include lankiness, a youthful build with youthful facial appearance, and a rounded body type with some degree of gynecomastia (increased breast tissue). Klinefelter's Syndrome is caused by a non-disjunction event during meiosis and affects 1 in 500 live male births. In all cases, however, such individuals are male and symptoms can be altered or treated using testosterone replacement.

Once considered a variation in Klinefelter's Syndrome, but no longer believed to be, is XXYY male syndrome occurring in 1 in 17,000 births. This exceedingly rare disorder results in hypogonadism. Common features of this disorder include tall stature, gynecomastia, trunkal obesity, and treatment again is aimed at hormonal replacement.

A frequently misunderstood and misrepresented syndrome is that of Jacob's Syndrome, also known as XYY syndrome. It is important to note XYY syndrome usually causes no unusual features, although such individuals may be slightly taller with slightly larger hands and feet than otherwise would be manifested. Such individuals are male and are capable of sexual development and able to conceive children. With no distinctive physical characteristics, the condition is usually only detected during genetic analysis for other reasons. Some have even questioned whether the term "syndrome" is appropriate for this condition because of its normal phenotype. The majority of individuals with this condition are unaware of the abnormality, the incidence being one in 1,000 male births. Such individuals may have increased learning difficulties and IQ scores of XYY boys average ten to fifteen points below their siblings. It should be emphasized this is a highly variable finding and once again, as in the other syndromes discussed, mosaicism is common. Unfortunately, many misconceptions abound concerning XYY syndrome, sometimes referred in the literature as a "supermale," with various criminal and aggressive behaviors blamed on it. For example, in Kenneth Royce's series of novels about the "XYY man," the stereotype figure William Spider Scott is responsible for highly skilled, though nonviolent cat burglaries as depicted in the United Kingdom's series television based on that book. In the film *Alien 3*, the protagonist lands on a planet populated by XYY criminals, once again implicating their proclivity for such crimes as rape, assault, and molestation. Even the popular 1960's series *Star Trek* was not immune from this unfortunate characterization of XYY syndrome, with one episode depicting the character Spock having an extra Y chromosome. The ship's physician, Dr. McCoy, was worried that Spock may be hypermasculine and unable to control emotional outbursts and violent behavior. More recently on an episode of *Law & Order*, in a crime involving a young boy with XYY chromosomes accused of beating to death another boy, experts were called in to testify that the XYY syndrome was more common amongst prison populations. Unfortunately, all these fictional descriptions are uncharacteristic of individuals with XYY chromosomes as there is no inherent increase in crime, misconduct, or aberrant sexual behaviors in these individuals. It should also be emphasized that XYY individuals are not more prone to homosexuality or towards transgender predisposition. The cause of XYY syndrome is, once again, a problem occurring at meiosis and is a random event and not inherited.

XXX or Triple X syndrome has sometimes been referred to as a version of female Klinefelter's and occurs in one in 1,000 live female births. Since only one X chromosome is "active" in females at any one time, there are no unusual clinical features in XXX syndrome. As adults, these individuals may be slightly taller than normal and experience some menstrual irregularities and in some cases, learning and speech development have been described. Such individuals are usually not sterile and have normal sexual development. This syndrome is rarely diagnosed and, as in the case of XYY syndrome, would only be diagnosed when genetic testing is carried out for other purposes.

There are many other syndromes involving increase numbers of either X or Y chromosomes. In all these rare syndromes, physical characteristics are variable. In Tetrasomy X or Quadruple X, individuals tend to have distinctive features, not unlike Down's syndrome. Treatment involves management of symptoms and support for learning disabilities and replacement with estrogen as all XXXX syndrome patients are female in phenotype. XXXXX or Pentasomy X, is associated with more severe disorders including defects in mental growth, motor retardation, facial features, including microcephale, micrognathia, and round face. The average IQ in Pentasomy X is between seventy and fifty-five. Again, all individuals with Pentasomy

X are phenotypically female, though the ovaries are abnormally shaped and the uterus is usually small. Finally, XXXXY Syndrome is extremely rare, occurring in only one in 85,000 to 100,000 males. This is considered a variant of Klinefelter's Syndrome by some and is usually accompanied by mental retardation. Once again, it occurs as a result of abnormalities occurring at the meiotic stage. The mental effects of 49 XXXXY Syndrome again vary but are often like Down Syndrome. Individuals are male but tend to exhibit infantile secondary sexual characteristics with sterility in adulthood.

Intersexuality can also occur when there are a normal number of XY or XX chromosomes. For example, with 46 XX intersex, the individual has the chromosomes of a woman with ovaries and uterus, but the external genitalia appear male. This can occur to a female fetus exposed to male hormones *in utero*. As a result, the labia fuses and the clitoris enlarges to appear like a penis. A primitive term "pseudohermaphroditism" is now replaced with the term "XX with virilization." There are multiple causes but the most common is referred to as congenital adrenal hyperplasia. In this case, the adrenal cortex produces excess hormones including testosterone, resulting in the virilization of the female. Other causes include exposure to male hormone or testosterone by the mother during pregnancy, male hormone producing tumors in the mothers such as ovarian tumors, and aromatase deficiency. Aromatase is an enzyme that converts male hormones to female hormones. When there is a deficiency in the female, especially at the time of puberty, the individual will begin to take on external genitalia with male characteristics. In the above cases, treatment is always directed at the cause.

Forty-six (46) XY interrex occurs in men with normal XY chromosomes but external genitalia either incompletely formed, ambiguous or clearly female. Testicles may be internal and either normal, malformed, or absent. Once called male "pseudohermaphroditism," this condition is now known as 46 XY with undervirilization. As in 46 XX intersex, 46 XY intersex has multiple possible causes including problems with the testicles, known as gonadal dysgenesis, problems with testosterone formation such as deficiencies in any of the enzymes required to form testosterones, and problems with the utilization of testosterone. 5-alpha reductase deficiency is a result in the latter. These individuals have normal amounts of testosterone but lack the enzyme needed to convert testosterone to dihydrotestosterone (DHT). The most common cause of 46 XY intersex is Androgen Insensitivity Syndrome (AIS). In this condition, the hormones are normal but the receptors to male hormones do not function properly. There are at least 150 different defects that can cause AIS, also referred to as testicular feminization. Once again, treatment is aimed at the exact cause of 46 XY intersex. Hormone replacement, enzymatic replacements, and, in some cases, surgical intervention may be needed.

True gonadal intersex referred to in the past as true hermaphroditism occurs in individuals who have both ovarian and testicular tissue. These persons may have XY chromosomes, XX chromosomes, or even both, which sometimes occurs in chimerism. External genitalia will be ambiguous or may appear male or female or both. Causes of gonadal intersex are unknown in most cases. Persons with true gonadal intersex usually choose to live exclusively as one sex or the other, with most opting for genital reconstruction surgery and hormone replacement.

The previously discussed chromosomal abnormalities and intersex disorders are all medical conditions diagnosed by either genetic or laboratory tests. They do not cause homosexuality or transgender dysmorphia. With the exception of true hermaphrodites, the individuals so affected are either male or female albeit sometimes with sexual ambiguity caused by either under virilization in males or virilization in females. They are all treatable at least to some extent and the individuals will lead lives of either a male or female. Treating hermaphrodites is a bit more complex. As mentioned, hermaphrodites usually choose to be either one sex or the other. Once that decision is made, treatment is directed at correcting the external anatomy to conform to the sex so chosen. The individual now leads the life of that sex.

Is Homosexuality Genetic?

Until 2007 most Americans believed "gay" people could change their sexual orientation if they wanted to. It appears that belief has now changed. A recent CNN poll showed that most Americans now feel homosexuality is an inborn trait. This should not be surprising. We have seen an insidious decline in morality for quite some time. Through the media, television, movies, and the Hollywood "lifestyle," people are desensitized to sins that were once repugnant. It is now common for couples to life together before marriage. Offensive language is now tolerated and accepted as are immodest apparel and nudity. Divorce no longer carries the stigma it once did. The gay "lifestyle" is now tolerated by society as an acceptable alternative and the CNN poll reflects that. Some of the secular literature refers to a "host" of studies demonstrating the biological causality of sexual orientation. So the question posed, "Is homosexuality genetic?"

Clearly, God's word condemns homosexuality. 1 Corinthians 6:9 condemns the effeminate and also states that homosexuals will not inherit the Kingdom of God. In both the Old and New Testaments, God has always condemned homosexuality. For example, the sins of Sodom and Gomorrah in Genesis 19, included sins of homosexuality and in 1 Timothy 1:10, homosexuals are linked to other sinful acts such as kidnapping, lying, and even murder that were "contrary to sound teaching." Paul's letter to the Roman Christians in Chapter 1:26-27 could not be any clearer in its condemnation of homosexuality:

> For this reason God gave them over to degrading passions; for women exchanged the natural function for that which is unnatural and in the same way also the men abandoned the natural function of the woman and burned in their desire toward one another, men with men committing indecent acts and receiving their own persons the due penalty of error.

If homosexuality has a genetic link and such individuals have no control over their behavior, this makes God a respecter of persons and causes those individuals to sin. This obviously is not the case. We will look at the "evidence" and "science" concerning studies that purport to "prove" the genetics of homosexuality. We do not believe these studies are valid but, even if a person was so inclined towards homosexual behavior, God certainly would not make someone behave in a way contrary to His word. One must choose to act on any sinful impulses or temptations, whether they are homosexual acts or other sinful acts such as those listed in 1 Timothy. We would also argue that the term "homosexual" is no different than the term "adulterer." It refers to those who continue to act in a sinful manner but does not describe that person, but rather the behavior. In fact, the use of the word "homosexual" as a noun describing a certain type of person rather than an adjective referring to specific characteristics dates from the beginning of the Twentieth Century, when British sexual liberators, Havelock Ellis and Edward Carpenter, argued that laws against same sex sexual activity should be dropped. Their arguing was based on the supposition that "homosexuals" were biologically different than heterosexual individuals.

In the last twenty-five years several studies have come forth that supposedly support the genetic predisposition of homosexuality. Attributing sexual orientation to genetics does have a certain appeal to some individuals. First, it attempts to naturalize lesbian and gay behavior. Secondly, it tries to "default the behavior." And thirdly, gay rights advocates would assert their activity is caused by certain "immutable characteristics," therefore, giving them more legal protection against discriminatory practices.

With these thoughts in mind, let's look at three studies that have been put forth as "proof" of a genetic basis for homosexuality. The most frequently studied report comes from the National Institute of Health under the direction of Dean Hamer. In Dr. Hamer's 1983 study, researchers claim to have found a DNA segment called a "marker" on the X chromosome of men that was found in most, though not all, homosexuals. Hamer's report, however, has been criticized from several points of view. First, his study was investigated by the Federal Office of Research Integrity, alleging one of his collaborators suppressed data that would have reduced the statistical significance of the reported results, though this investigation was "quietly dropped without any formal resolution." Secondly, Hamer and his colleagues did not apparently feel it necessary to check whether any straight men of the homosexual families shared the same marker in question on their chromosomes. Even more troubling was the definition of who was gay used by Hamer and his associates. Hamer used an extremely conservative estimate of 2% for the prevalence of homosexual activity in American man; increasing the value to the "more acceptable" 5% to 10% reduces or even eliminates statistical significance in his study. The reason quoted by Dr. Hamer for using this number was to "work only with real gay men, that is men who have never veered from their preference for men and sexual fantasies or activities." Hamer's results are controversial and an independent study of gay siblings did not reproduce his findings and, as a result, no study including Hamer's can support the claim that any single gene can determine sexual orientation other than the X and Y chromosomes.

In another study sometimes cited, neurophysiologist Simon LeVay examined the hypothalamus in the brains of gay men and claimed their "intersittal nuclei" were smaller than those of straight men. Unfortunately, LeVay's observations were made on brains of cadavers and evidence of sexual orientation was entirely circumstantial. Also, all of the gay men died of AIDS, which can affect the brain structures and furthermore, in some of LeVay's gay samples, the structures were larger than the "straight" ones inspected, confirming no basis for deciding whether a given person in life had been "gay" or "straight."

The third study frequently postulated "proving" a genetic basis for homosexuality involves the study of twins by Michael Bailey and Richard Pillard at Northwestern University and Boston University School of Medicine. They found, for adoptive and non-twin brothers of gay men, about 10% were also gay, roughly that attributed often to the general population, whereas the rate of homosexuality doubled for paternal twins (22%) and for identical twins it was 52%. This, however, could be interpreted as showing strong environmental factors in play and not necessary genetics. It would not be surprising that a larger population of identical twins would have similar behaviors, since they would be raised in a same or nearly same environment. In fact, the argument could be: Why are not 100% of identical twins gay if indeed there is a true genetic causation in homosexuality since identical twins share exactly the same chromosomal material. Their study was further criticized because study participants were "recruited" through advertisements in gay literature, thus all those responding to the study were predisposed to be more public about their sexuality. As a result, men with gay brothers might well have been more likely to participate than men with straight brothers in this particular study. Also, if identical twins were both gay, they might be more subject to volunteer for such a study.

Based upon these three frequently cited studies, the scientific evidence for a biologic basis of sexual orientation remains weak at best. This, in no way, however, should be justification for violent discrimination against those who call themselves "gay" or "homosexual," anymore so than violence against any sinner.

Transexualism and Transgenderism

Just as in homosexuality where genetic-basis has been sought, attempts have been made also to find a biologic or genetic basis for transgenderism. Actually, more to the point, a genetic basis has been sought for transsexualism. Transgenderism is an umbrella term for a wide range of behaviors including transvestitism and transsexualism. A transsexual individual seeks medical treatment for sex reassignment surgery because what has been termed "gender identity disorder" or gender dysphoria. Transvestite individuals, on the other hand, primarily are interested in cross-dressing and usually do not seek sexual reassignment. So is there is a genetic basis for transsexualism? Certainly there is no abnormality in the sex chromosomes of these individuals. Recently however, researchers from Prince Henry's Institute of Medical Research in Melbourne, Australia have been studying gender dysphoria. Out of 112 male transsexuals studied, most were found to have a longer androgen receptor gene. The hypothesis, according to Lauren Hare of Prince Henry's Institute, was that this receptor might "reduce testosterone action and under masculinize the brain during fetal development." This lone study, which is weak evidence at best, does not "prove" gender dysphoria to be necessarily biologic, the incident of which is estimated to be 1 in 12,000 men and 1 in 30,000 women, according to Harry Benjamin of the International Gender Dysphoria Association. Dr. Lori Kohler, a primary care physician for about 100 transgender patients in California, has stated, "medically there is no explanation" (for gender dysphoria). "There are lots and lots of theories in the psychology and psychiatry worlds. It is probably much like gay or lesbian. No one can explain it. It is just something that exists." Certainly, one has to believe there is a strong environmental influence in transgender individuals.

Today, transsexual individuals have the option of surgical reconstruction, also known as sex reassignment surgery. This of course, does not change the sex of the individual but only the external anatomy. Most centers performing sex reassignment surgery and therapy follow guidelines proposed by Dr. Henry Benjamin. Before surgery is performed, transsexual individuals are usually required to live as members of their target sex for at least a year prior to surgery, the so-called real life test or real-life experience. This "waiting period" is obviously suggested in order to prevent persons from seeking transition surgery to change identity or where transition surgery is ill-advised, as in the case of those who are cross dressers but not transsexuals. Dr. Benjamin's standards have been criticized from both sides. The transsexual community points to meta-analysis that show serious regrets occurring in less than 1% of transsexual men and less than 2% of transsexual women. In a report from the United Kingdom, opposite conclusions have been found. In fact, the UK *Guardian Newspaper* states there is "no conclusive evidence that sex change operations improve the lives of transsexuals, with many people remaining severely distressed and even suicidal after the operation." Their conclusion, taken from over 100 international medical studies of postoperative transsexuals, found "no robust scientific evidence that gender reassignment surgery is clinically effective."

Does the Bible condemn transsexualism, transvestitism, and cross-dressing? We believe it does. In discussing those who are unrighteous and would not inherit the Kingdom of God, 1 Corinthians 6:9 includes those who are effeminate along with homosexuals, adulterers, idolaters, and fornicators. These sins include those who are considered immoral in verse 18 of that same Chapter. So, can a person help the way he feels? Transsexuals state they feel trapped in a body of a gender they don't feel part of. Would God condemn someone for engaging in behavior he could not help? Certainly not! Transsexual behavior can be avoided, although a biological cause cannot be totally dismissed. We live in a time when a biologic or genetic predisposition is being discovered for a lot of actions condemned by God, but can nonetheless be controlled. It is our belief that transsexuals can control behavior that would result in sin. We should emphasize this is not to condemn those with true genetic disorders, discussed earlier in this chapter, that result in sexual ambiguity. Transgenderism is not sexual ambiguity. We must trust in God and trust in His laws. True happiness comes in obeying the will of God, looking forward to our reward, which is not of an earthly basis.

Genetics and Behavior

The progressive or enlightened view is now to consider genetics along with up bringing, race, and socioeconomic factors as causes of aberrant or sinful behavior, thus granting us freedom from accountability. Over the last fifteen years a genetic "link" has been "discovered" for attention-deficit disorder, alcoholism, smoking, obesity, pedophilia, depression, gambling, violent aggression, anxiety, drug addiction, obsessive-compulsive disorder, schizophrenia, impulsivity, and as mentioned homosexuality and sexual orientation. In fact, it is hard to find a behavior that is not "explained" by genetics. Recently, Swedish researchers at the Karolinska Institute discovered a gene, the Allele 334, they feel may be responsible for men cheating on their wives! Dean Hamer, the same person who discovered the "homosexual gene" discussed earlier has even found a genetic basic for our belief in God!

Does man then have a choice in his behavior? If he does not, then God's Word is a sham and we have no "right" to prosecute evil doers such as rapists, murderers, thieves, pedophiles, and such like. Civilization understands we must have some standards and society seems to acknowledge the above behaviors are wrong and controllable, but when it comes to sexual orientation, society holds that man has no control. The truth is man can and must control not only his behavior but his thoughts as well (Matthew 15:19 and 2 Corinthians 10:5). Man certainly has a free will. James 1:13-15 states,

> Let no one say when he is tempted, "I am being tempted by God;" for God cannot be tempted by evil and He Himself does not tempt anyone. But each one is tempted when he is carried away and enticed by his own lust. Then when lust has conceived, it gives birth to sin; and when sin is accomplished it brings forth death.

The problem is man has turned his back on the standard we are to use in determining right and wrong, the Bible.

This is not to totally ignore the importance of genetics in our lives. We are born with certain traits, keeping in mind less than 10% of human genes are expressed. Environment also plays a role in the "waking up" of these traits and though traits may be genetic, behavior is not. For example, a child born to alcoholic parents and with the genetics for alcoholism will be more likely to become an alcoholic than a child not born to this environment or trait. Still that child will not become alcoholic if he or she never takes the first drink and, even if he does, that behavior, that is the drinking behavior, can be controlled.

What about the Christian attitude?

Homosexuality and transgenderism as we have seen are sins and violate God's law. This is vitally important because Romans 6:23 states, "The wages of sin is death," not physical death though all mankind must die, but spiritual death, that is separation from God. Sin is lawlessness (1 John 3:4) and no one born of God practices sin. That is not to say that none of us falters at times. In fact if we say we have no sin, "we deceive ourselves and the truth is not in us" (1 John 1:8). It is only through Jesus Christ that man can have his sins removed. Again in 1 John 2:2 the apostle says, "He Himself (Christ) is the propitiation for our sins and not ours only but for those of the whole world."

The Christian response to the homosexual should be one of love and compassion. We should attempt to bring him/her to Christ, as we would any sinner, understanding that we are all imperfect servants and fall short of the glory of God (Romans 3:23). Christians cannot be discriminators of sin. Homosexuality, though wrong, is no worse a sin than stealing, lying, or covetousness. Sometimes confronting sin can be difficult, yet what could be more moral or ethical than to save someone's soul? It is a bit of paradox

Sexual Ambiguity and Chromosomal Abnormalities

but many people in the "gay" community are otherwise very moral. We all have friends, fellow workers, or schoolmates who are "gay." On a personal level, some of the most caring, loving, and compassionate people we have known lead a "gay" lifestyle. Our society has accepted this and as long as people are not causing others harm, it is considered rude and discriminatory to refer to homosexuals as sinners.

Proverbs 14:9 states, "fools mock at sin." To call something sin is now considered almost silly by our society, yet sin is not funny and will cause a soul to be lost if unrepented of. It is therefore right and even moral to condemn the homosexual lifestyle. God would have all to come to repentance (2 Peter 3:9). Paul in 1 Corinthians 10:13 writes, "No temptation has overtaken you but such as is common to man; and God is faithful who will not allow you to be tempted beyond what you are able; but with the temptation will provide the way of escape that you may be able to endure it." It is obligatory for all of us to find that avenue of escape no matter what sins we are tempted to commit.

What about happiness? Some have stated they can only be truly happy living a transgender or homosexual life. They fail to understand that God has never promised us happiness, if that happiness depends on violating God's laws! For example, using the same reasoning as above, fornicators, idolaters, pedophiles, and murderers may justify their behaviors. This simply makes a mockery of God's Word. We can and must control the behaviors that are described as sinful in God's Word. We are not doing anyone a favor when we simply accept a sinful lifestyle. Furthermore, Ephesians 5:11 reads, "An do not participate in the unfruitful deeds of darkness but instead even expose them." We cannot fellowship sin.

It is only through Jesus that any sinner can have his or her sins forgiven. John the Baptist understood this when, seeing Jesus in Bethany, he eloquently exclaimed, "Behold the Lamb of God who takes away the sin of the world" (John 1:29). It is only through Jesus Christ that we have remission on sins and it is through faith and obedience that our sins are forgiven (1 John 2:3; Matthew 28:19-20; Mark 16:16). Through an obedient faith we put on Christ in baptism (Galatians 3:27), thus having our sins forgiven (Acts 2:38).

Once receiving the remission on sins, we cannot go on sinning and be pleasing to God. Jesus told the adulteress woman in John 8:11 to "sin no more." In Romans 6:12 we are told to "not let sin reign in your mortal body that you should obey its lust." One cannot call oneself a Christian and continue to lead a sinful life such as homosexuality; they are mutually exclusive. Christians are and must be dogmatic when it concerns the law of Christ. We are not dogmatic for the sake of dogmatism; we are simply concerned for the souls of all men looking to ourselves first. It is out of love that Christians wish for all to come to the knowledge of Christ.

Chapter 7
Genetic Testing and Gene Therapy

Beloved I pray that in all respects you may prosper and be in good health, just as your soul prospers (3 John 2).

Probably the most promising area of medical research today is gene therapy, although to date, no practical use has been perfected. There have been several attempts but they have failed. Still, the future of gene therapy is extremely promising and impacts virtually every disease known to man.

Gene therapy, different from genetic engineering, involves replacing an abnormal gene with a "normal" one. We all have at least one or more genes that are imperfect and can result in disease. In fact, most all of disease or illness have some genetic component in man, save for trauma. The difficulty comes in identifying the gene or genes responsible for the disease through genetic testing, then replacing those genes with normal ones.

Gene testing is already in use with the field evolving rapidly. To date, there are predictive tests for such cancers as Wilm's tumor, familial adenomatus polyposus, hereditary non-polyposus colon cancer, and the BRCA-1 gene mutation, which predisposes one to breast cancer and ovarian cancer. Since no curative gene therapy exists for these cancers, positive tests create opportunities for counseling and early intervention in high-risk patients. Still gene testing has its limitations and its challenges, as many diseases go as yet unidentified genetically, and some diseases involve multiple chromosomes. Furthermore, predictive tests deal in probabilities and not certainties, as those found with genetic mutations may never express the disease tested. Genetic testing can also effect the emotions of those tested when certain mutations are identified. Anxiety, depression, confusion, insomnia, and interpersonal and interfamily relationships can be affected by such tests. Someone who elects to have genetic testing needs to consider these factors as well as with whom he or she will share the results and how such sharing may affect one's relationships. The issue of privacy is of concern as to who will have access to such information. For example, will such information impact the ability to obtain health insurance, employability for certain jobs, or even the permissibility to adopt. The Genetic Information Non-discrimination Act was recently passed by Congress and signed into Law by President George W. Bush. This bill is designed to protect individuals with known genetic diseases from being denied insurance coverage. The drawback is the increased premiums that will be passed on to individuals that do not have genetic diseases. Some have proposed a ban on what is called "medical underwriting" and instead propose requiring a community rating of all people within the same category, the exception being to permit insurance to surcharge individuals involved in risky activity within their own individual self control such as smoking. Other ethical questions relate to the use of therapeutic cloning as discussed in Chapter 4 for treatment of genetic disorders.

Before leaving the topic of genetic testing, a word of caution needs to be given. There are many "retail" genetic laboratories across the country for which there is little regulation. These labs have become very popular and, in fact, *TIME* magazine named "23 and ME," a DNA testing service, its invention of the year for 2008. For $399 you can collect a sample of saliva and test more than 90 traits and conditions ranging from "baldness to blindness." Though there are other "retail" labs, *TIME* magazine picked "23 and ME" (heavily funded by GOOGLE) because of their superior marketing. Critics of "retail" labs have pointed out the uncertainty of the results since many diseases are stimulated by several genes and since less than 1/10 of our 20,000 genes can be correlated with any condition, it becomes almost impossible to predict what genes will be expressed.

New York and California have attempted to ban "retail" DNA labs because of their improper licensing but so far there is no legislation prohibiting them. One argument against regulation made by such labs is that they do not "test patient genomes" but just analyze them. It should be noted these labs are different from true clinical labs for which there is regulation. At this time the Department of Health and Human Services has formed an advisory committee to look into the matter of regulation to insure adequacy and regulation of quality assurance, how such test are introduced into clinical practice, understanding of genetic test results by health care providers, and continued availability an quality of testing for rare diseases. Still at present, "retail" genetic labs are not required to enroll in programs that assess their proficiency in test performance.

An example of how some of these "retail" genetic tests are marketed is the analysis of the ACTN3 gene, which has been linked to athletic ability published in study from Australia in 2003. This test is now marketed to parents to help ascertain certain athletic traits their children may or may not have. Carl Foster, co-author of the afore mentioned study, points out that results are not always valid and a better predictor of a child's athletic abilities is just to "line them up with their classmates for a race and see which ones are the faster." The point is, one has to be careful with some of the genetic labs that are out there and be cautious of the results obtained. Nonetheless, parents are spending $149 per test to determine if their child is more likely to be sprinters or power lifters!

Genetic Therapy

We are on the precipice of an explosion in genetic therapy. As a result, life expectancy may well increase. This in itself poses more questions. For example, will we be able financially to care for the elderly as that sector of our population grows? Furthermore, will genetic therapy not only increase quantity of life, but will it increase quality of life? At this time, we do not have all the answers to these questions.

The beginning of gene therapy is to identify the defective gene through gene testing discussed earlier. With the human genetic project, we now have identified genes responsible for over 4,000 disorders including cystic fibrosis, Tay-Sach's disease, Alzheimer's disease, colon cancer, breast cancer, heart disease, diabetes, and many, many more.

As mentioned, gene therapy presently is a research tool and there are no FDA approved treatments as of yet. The first clinical trials using genetic therapy began in 1990. In 1999, gene therapy suffered a significant setback with the death of eighteen-year-old Jesse Gelzinger who was participating in gene therapy for a disorder known as Ornithine Transcarboxylase deficiency (OTCD). Jesse died from multiple organ failures four days after starting treatment, believed to be attributed to a severe immune response to the adenovirus carrier for the genetic therapy. Another major blow came in January of 2003 when the FDA halted gene therapy trials using retroviral vectors in blood stem cells. This action took place after it was learned a French gene therapy trial resulted in a leukemia-like condition when treatment was carried out for combined immunodeficiency disease (bubble baby syndrome) in two children, who subsequently died. Still, ongoing research is being carried out, as we shall see at the end of this chapter.

Current research methods involve "swapping" a normal gene for an abnormal gene through homologous recombination, which involves inserting the normal gene into a nonspecific location within the genome to replace a non-functional gene. This is the most common approach currently being used and results hopefully in the repairing of the abnormal gene through a "selective reverse mutation" and altering the regulation of that particular gene.

In order to swap or insert a normal gene into the genome and replace the abnormal one, a carrier vehicle or molecule must be used, the most common being a virus. Viruses can deliver their own gene to somatic cells of the human body. This is how they impart their illness. Science has tried to take advantage of this and use viruses as vectors to transfer the normal human genes. Retroviruses, adenoviruses, adeno associated viruses, and herpes viruses have all been used in research. Non-viral delivery systems include direct introduction of DNA into target cells, using an artificial lipid sphere and chemically linking DNA to a molecule to bind with certain receptors. Also, researchers are experimenting with an "artificial chromosome," or 47th if you will, introducing it into the target cells.

At this point a brief word should be said about the relationship between cloning, stem cell research, and gene therapy. There is considerable overlap in how these techniques are and will be used therapeutically. For example, stem cells may be "cloned" and these stem cells may be used to treat genetic abnormalities.

Several problems must be overcome for gene therapy to ever become successful. First, therapeutic DNA must be more long-lived and stable than is presently the case. Currently, the rapid developing nature of DNA prevents gene therapy from long-term goals with patients requiring multiple rounds of therapy. Second, overcoming the body's immune response to the viral vector used is a major problem. The body will "reject" foreign DNA (whether viral or not), such as seen in transplant cases. This "toxic" inflammatory response is very detrimental. Also, the viral vector itself used to transfer genetic material could lead to disease. Finally, another hurdle in gene therapy is treating diseases caused by multiple genes, which are many. For example, common disorders such as heart disease, high blood pressure, Alzheimer's, dementia, and arthritis are all caused by a combined effect of various genes. Treating these multi-genetic and multi-factorial problems is especially difficult.

Despite these obstacles, gene therapy research presses on and medical scientists perceive a bright future. Research is worldwide, taking place in such places as London, Houston, Washington, D.C., Cincinnati, Los Angeles, Detroit, and many other places, looking at cures for genetic diseases such as Leber's congenital amaurosis (an inherited cause of childhood blindness), lung cancer, melanoma, acute myeloid leukemia, Parkinson's disease, Huntington's chorea, thalassemia, cystic fibrosis, X-length severe acquired immunodeficiency syndrome, and sickle cell disease, just to mention a few.

Are there ethical considerations to consider in gene therapy? Possibly so. For example, who defines what is normal and what is a disability or disorder. Also, some may want to "change" genetics for things that are clearly not disease, such as stature, color of hair, color of skin, and color of eyes. Given today's economic woes, some even question whether it is appropriate to spend vast amounts of money in genetic research. Another ethical question involves "germ line" genetic therapy done on eggs or sperm to prevent transmission of "traits" for future generations. Should this be done? Who would want to make such decisions concerning this? The final question and possibly the most important from our discussion, pertains to the use of genetic testing in utero for the purposes of early termination of pregnancy, which is already being done. As we can see, genetic therapy poses some significant moral and ethical questions, which hopefully science will address and hopefully consider God's word in answering such questions.

Chapter 8
End of Life Issues

."... For bodily discipline is only of little profit, but godliness is profitable for all things, since it holds promise for the present life and also for the life to come" (1 Timothy 4:8).

Recently, researchers believe they have identified the fundamental cause of aging, published in the journal "Cell." This study looked at a group of genes known as the Sirtuins that are involved in the aging process. Researchers have known that Sirtuins regulate cellular responses to stress and ensure damaged DNA is not propagated in the cell. As a result, the Sirtuins have been considered critical regulators in aging and even in controlling cancer. Scientists are now beginning to look at mechanisms that affect the Sirtuins in order to prolong life expectancy. For example, although seemingly a paradox, starving decelerates the aging process by some unknown action on the Sirtuin genes. Recently, a chemical known as Resveratrol, present in red wine and grapes, was found to mimic the affects of very low-calorie diets as were flavones found abundantly in olive oil. Though of no practical use yet (for example, Resveratrol is very unstable and goes away when wine is exposed to air for more than one day), eventually these chemicals may aid in the prolongation of life by their affect on the Sirtuin genes.

Who doesn't want to live long? Most do, especially if that life is still sound of body and mind. We have looked in this book at promising medical technologies that hope to expand life on this earth. There is certainly nothing wrong with wanting to live a long time in the world but Christians understand that this is a temporal world and our goal is to "lay up for ourselves treasures in Heaven, where moth and dust will not corrupt" (Matthew 6:20).

Still, no matter how long one does live, the Scriptures say it is appointed unto man to die, then comes the judgment (Hebrews 9:27). But when does death occur? This may sound like a simplistic question but volumes are written in the medical literature attempting to identify the moment of death. In fact, it may not be an easy thing to identify the exact point of death. The Bible defines death as a separation of the soul and the body. Never do the Scriptures refer to death as annihilation. The Scriptures actually define three kinds of death: (1) Physical, or the separation of soul and spirit (James 2:26); (2) Spiritual death, the separation of man from God (Matthew 8:22; Ephesians 2:1; Colossians 2:13; and 1 Timothy 5:26); and (3) Eternal death, or eternal separation from God because of unrepented sins (Matthew 10:28, 24, 41 and 46; Revelation 2:11; 14:9-11; 20:11-15; and Isaiah 66:22). For our purposes, we will discuss the first death, the separation of the body from the spirit. We must ask, once again, though, when does this moment occur? The fact that it does is certain but when? Just as in Chapter 2, in our discussion of personhood, man may never be able to precisely identify the exact moment of death. God will know, and surely the individual herself or himself will know. Nonetheless, man has attempted to identify and define the moment of death.

Traditionally, death has been defined when the heart and the lungs have irreversibly ceased to function. Loss of permanent consciousness may or may not have already occurred. Sometimes, the interval between loss of consciousness and cardiopulmonary failure may have been minutes or even days, especially with the advent of artificial respiration and resuscitation. With organ transplant becoming prevalent in the late Twentieth Century, a more precise definition of death was needed as to not delay unnecessarily the determination of death in order to procure vital organs. The so-called "dead donor rule" forbids the procurement of organs before the donor is "dead." Otherwise, it would be judged a homicide.

In a move to redefine the traditional view of death, two landmark reports were generated, the first in 1968 being the Harvard Medical School ad hoc committee and the second in 1981 the Presidential Committee "Defining Death." With the second committee, the Uniform Determination of Death Act (UDDA) came into being and is now used by all 50 states and the District of Columbia to define death.

In the UDDA, death is now considered to occur when either cardiopulmonary functions have ceased or when brain activity has permanently ended. It is important to note in this definition that a person can now be declared dead, even if cardiopulmonary functions were still active. In other words, if a person's entire brain is deemed nonfunctional and life is being maintained by artificial means, that individual can still be declared dead.

Some have argued the whole brain standard of death, as this has been called, does not go far enough. They want to define death as a cessation of "higher brain functions," meaning irreversible loss of the capacity for consciousness. Often, this standard is met before whole brain function has stopped (lower brain or brainstem function can continue, thus cardiopulmonary function continues). A person in a coma or permanent vegetative state (PVS) meets a higher brain definition of death but not a whole brain definition of death. This higher brain definition of death puts us on somewhat of a slippery slope because it is sometimes very difficult to determine if future capacity for consciousness exists. Meaningful and functional return to consciousness occurs with regularity from PVS and also from the minimal conscience state. Such was the case of Zac Dunlap in November 2007. Mr. Dunlap had been pronounced dead on November 19, 2007 at the United Regional Healthcare System in Wichita Falls, Texas. Mr. Dunlap's family had already approved the procurement of his organs, when paying their last respects, they noticed movement of a hand and foot. Obviously, Mr. Dunlap was not dead and 48 days later he was allowed to return home. Clearly, this case indicates the imprecision of determining death.

Patients in PVS and minimal consciousness with minimal or no motor function can be extremely difficult to evaluate for level of consciousness as well as their cognitive ability to perceive and understand commands. By using functional magnetic resonance imaging, Owen et.al. in 2007 showed supplementary motor area activity during tennis imagery was identical in PVS patients to that of healthy individuals. This means a patient in PVS who appears unaware of the environment may in fact be fully aware and cognitively intact but unable to show any response to stimuli. Also in 2007, Schiff et. al. reported a severely brain injured patient was able to recover spoken language and oral feeding after undergoing deep brain stimulation. One can therefore, not equate a PVS state with death unless one allows for a dead person to talk!

It is therefore, very important to understand the difference between a comatose person and those with minimal consciousness or in a PVS with those who are whole brain dead. Those persons with whole brain death cannot sustain "life" without an artificial breathing machine, as there is no brain function including the brain stem while the person in PVS is alive but will die without nourishment, usually through a feeding tube such as a PEG (percutanious endoscopic gastrotomy) tube.

Some people, specifically Charles Culvert and Bernard Gert, have defined death as "the permanent cessation of the functioning of the organism as a whole." This refers to the integrated function of the organism with most, if not all, the important sub systems working. Death in this sense is from a more biologic perspective. Current definitions of death are compatible with this point of view but higher brain standard is not as evident with this approach, especially when the person is in a permanent vegetative state. The mind may be gone but brainstem functions continue, thus the individual organism is "alive."

Of course, humans are not just "organisms" but persons with the capacity for human thought. Conscious thought is vital, even essential to a living person. It might follow that a being that has lost personality and consciousness for all intents and purposes is dead. In other words, when we no longer know we exist, is there a point to existing at all? If life is defined as the capacity for consciousness, then death occurs when such capacity is lost.

There are, however, significant problems with this loss of person definition that cannot be resolved. First, if this definition is used, people in PVS have two deaths, in essence. First, a person dies and then the organism. This is an untenable position! Also, life as defined as loss of consciousness begs the question, what about the organism or organisms that do not or have never had such capacity? Are they not living beings? Furthermore, newborn babies lack the psychological capacity for rationality and self-awareness, but only the most extreme individuals would deny they are persons. Think about it, if we cannot exist as non-persons, then we need not exist as a newborn! This would mean newborns are just "organic" pre-persons, which is nonsensical. Finally, what about the severely disabled at birth? Are they not human persons too? It is our belief that an individual is dead when either cardiopulmonary functions permanently stop or when the whole brain ceases to function. Any other definition places us in a precarious spot. This is most certainly the case for the individual in a permanent vegetative state of which, at any one time, 19,000 to 35,000 exist in the United States. How are these to be treated? Unfortunately, in the case of Terri Schiavo, our government has seemed to accept a higher brain definition of death, even though this is not the law. As you may recall, Ms. Schiavo was involved in a severe brain injury in 1990 and lived some 15 years in a vegetative state, dependent on artificial hydration and nutrition to live. In September of 2004, the Supreme Court of Florida issued a ruling that would eventually allow, in March of 2005, Michael Shiavo to remove Terri's PEG tube, essentially allowing her to starve to death. On March 31, 2005, Terri Schiavo, nearly thirteen days after removal of her PEG tube, died.

There is also a condition known as the "locked in state" and occurs when severe and permanent paralysis exists yet consciousness is not affected. Probably the most common cause of the "locked in state" is amyotrophic lateral sclerosis or Lou Gehrig's disease. These individuals maintain normal levels of consciousness, easily determined by EEGs, MRIs, etc., yet have lost all motor function. They maintain cardiac function but pulmonary function is maintained by artificial respirations and feedings occur through feeding tubes. Such people are living individuals and capable of conscious thought and, in some cases, extraordinary conscious thought, as evidenced by Stephen Hawkins, the eminent physicist and author of *A Brief History of Time*.

The question remains: How are Christians to approach death? Is it all right to sign a Living Will? Can a Christian refuse "heroic measures" to maintain life? Can Christians remove feeding tubes and respirators from persons who are "whole brain dead" and even more so, can Christians remove such devices from those who are in a "permanent vegetative state"?

As mentioned in earlier chapters, the guiding principle in answering the above questions is do they involve the taking of innocent life, so strongly forbidden in all of God's word? Suicide is the taking of innocent life and is condemned in God's word, but is it suicide to refuse a treatment that might prolong life but not necessarily give hope for a permanent cure? We believe there is nothing wrong, for example, in a Christian signing a Living Will, keeping in mind there are several different types of Living Wills, one of which totally refutes any form of artificial means of life, while others may specify exactly which types of life support may be opted for. Choosing which if any living will a person wishes to sign may depend on what type of artificial life supports one wishes to refuse as well as what the circumstances are. For example, a person may not want to be kept alive by "extraordinary" means if their disability is permanent. Using a mechanical ventilator or respirator may be very desirable if a person has pneumonia but not so desirable when one has suffered a "massive stroke". The dilemma for a physician and patient can often be determining "permanent and irreversible" disability from a temporary state. This is not always obvious. Likewise, a feeding tube may be very appropriate after major surgery but not so in the case of a "terminal illness" such as cancer. Here again, determining what is "terminal" is not always so evident. In opting for a "living will" also known as "an advanced medical directive" a person is asking for do not resuscitate orders (DNR). Cardiopulmonary resuscitation (CPR) involves electric shock, insertion of a respiratory tube for mechanical ventilation, injection of medication into the heart, and in extreme cases, open chest heart massage, and would be done emergently after cardiac or pulmonary arrest. In asking for a DNR order, an individual is saying they do not want any of these procedures performed on them although DNR orders can be specific as to which procedures the individual wishes to refuse. Any adult of sound mind can ask for DNR orders and a physician is obligated to honor them. The most appropriate scenarios for DNR orders are in the cases of "terminal illness" when resuscitation would only prolong life for a short time at best. Unfortunately, sometimes at this state in a person's life he or she may not be mentally competent to make such important medical decisions. This is when a Durable Power of Attorney may be appropriate. With a Durable Power of Attorney an individual selects a person ahead of time to act in their best interest should they become mentally incapacitated. In this case it is very important to select a person who is competent and trustworthy understanding the power of attorney does not go into effect until a doctor certifies mental incompetence and the power of attorney ends at the patient's death. Laws regarding power of attorney may differ from state to state.

The question arises is it ethical for Christians to ask for DNR orders? Is it committing suicide to refuse resuscitation? Before the advent of defibrillators and mechanical ventilators in the 1960s, these questions were not relevant but more advanced cardiac life supports can now prolong life that in the past would have ended possibly prematurely. Sometimes though, CPR prolongs life but not necessarily improves quality of life. Hence, the DNR orders become important because without it health care providers are required to use all possible efforts to resuscitate a person in cardiopulmonary arrest. Asking for DNR orders is not the same as suicide in the case of a terminal illness and is not the taking of innocent life. Asking for DNR order, in fact, relieves the burden on family members and is quite appropriate. Having said this, there certainly may be scenarios where DNR orders may be unethical especially when CPR is used for illnesses that are not of a permanent nature. In any event, at the end of ones life if one does not choose to be "kept alive" by artificial means, we do not believe this violates the principle of the taking of innocent life. Each individual has the right to die a natural death with dignity but we do not believe any one else has that right over such a person.

Clearly communication is key when signing living wills, advanced medical directives, and do not resuscitate orders. One must be explicit in determining, as best they can, what their wishes are. Too often we have seen cases when the family is left in decision making processes because the patient did not make it clear what their desires where before they became mentally incapable of doing so.

There are times in the case of a terminal patient when Hospice care is not only appropriate but recommended. The term Hospice, first coined by Dame Cicely Saunders in London, applies to care for the terminally ill. Opting for Hospice care implies a change philosophically by the patient and the caregiver. Hospice care philosophically accepts death as the final stage of life. As a result the goal of Hospice care is not prolonging life but improving quality of life by treating pain and managing symptoms to keep the patient as comfortable and alert as possible so their last days may end with dignity and quality. Hospice care is person centered and not disease centered. In most cases patients in Hospice no longer are hospitalized for care and would have DNR orders. With Hospice care the physician is not expecting the life of the patient to last more than one year, but certainly patients can opt out of Hospice care if the prognosis improves. As Christian physicians we believe Hospice care, in the appropriate setting, is beneficial and frequently under utilized. Death is indeed the final stage of life and something none of us can escape. Christians have no reason to fear death. The apostle Paul felt to die was his gain (Phil. 1:21) realizing his citizenship was in heaven (Phil. 3:21) and to die "in the Lord" was to be blessed (Rev. 14:13).

A precarious situation is what to do when life supports have already been instituted? If whole function has ceased, removing artificial devices is not the taking of innocent life. Life, in our opinion, has already ceased, but what about those in a permanent vegetative state? We do not believe man has the right to stop the feeding of these persons and to do so is the taking of innocent life, clearly condemned in the word of God.

There are endless numbers of scenarios that might occur with difficult decisions necessary. It is not in the scope of this book to discuss every such scenario, but in all cases Christians must turn to God and must use wisdom and prayer to answer such questions.

As mentioned in the beginning of the chapter, bodily strength is of little value when compared to spiritual strength and vitality. All of our bodies, if we live long enough, will eventually deteriorate and die. There is nothing man can do to prevent the inevitable. What man can and must do is set our goals and standards on things spiritual. We will be given a new body, according to 1 Corinthians 15, at the resurrection. What this body will look like, we cannot know, but we do know it will be an immortal body for this mortality must put on immortality which will not decay as our fleshly bodies do. For those who have obeyed God's word, this new body will dwell with the Father and Son and Holy Spirit in Heaven forever. For those who have not obeyed God, there dwelling will be with Satan and his angels forever. Which place would you rather dwell? Jesus says we must come to Him in order to have eternal life.

Epilogue

Before ending this book we thought it would be interesting to look at a few current headlines that were relevant to our theme as we come to print. The topics we have discussed will be obvious in these stories.

Dateline, January 28, 2009. "Birth of Octuplets Rattle Experts"

Nadya Suleman, a mother of six children already, gave birth to 8 more children on January 26, 2009. During the births, which were by caesarean section, she was attended by forty-six physicians and medical staff. The children were six boys and two girls and weighed between 1 lb., 8 oz. and 3 lbs., 4 oz. All were reported alive and doing well. Later it was revealed by Nadya's mother, Angela, that not only were all eight of these children produced by *in vitro* fertilization but so were the other six. Angela Suleman believes her daughter, who is unwed, is obsessed with having children. It is estimated the medical cost incurred by each child will be $400,000 or approximately $3.2 million for all eight. Ms. Suleman has hired a marketing firm to "sell" her story in order to defray some of the cost. Ms. Suleman has been criticized for having so many children, for having so many *in vitro* implantations, for not aborting or removing some of the children when it became obvious they were developing *in utero* and trying to "cash in" on her notoriety. Needless to say some medical experts are disturbed that a doctor or fertility clinic would have implanted so many embryos to begin with. Do you see any ethical problems in this story?

Dateline, January 24, 2009. "President Obama Resends the 'Mexico City Policy'"

On January 24, newly inaugurated President Barack Obama ordered the Secretary of State to publish a memorandum which immediately overturned the so called "Mexico City Policy" instituted by President Ronald Reagan in 1984. That policy prohibited non-governmental organizations (NGOs) from receiving federal funds if such funds were to be used "to pay for the performance of abortions as a method of family planning, or to motivate or coerce any person to practice abortions." This policy was in effect from 1984 until 1993 when it was first rescinded by President Clinton then reinstated by President George W. Bush in 2001. President Obama considers the restrictions in the "Mexico City Policy" "unwarranted" and "undermine efforts to promote safe and effective voluntary planning programs in foreign nations." Are there any moral or ethical concerns with this action?

As we come to the end of the first decade of the 21st Century, the afore scenarios allude to current potential ethical concerns discussed in this book. No doubt the 21st Century will continue to raise more ethical problems, some we cannot even anticipate at this time. Generations past had to deal with "new" medical treatments such as blood transfusions and organ transplants. In fact, some sects such as the Jehovah's Witness reject these treatments on ethical grounds, though we believe there biblical concerns are not founded in Scripture. The next generations will encounter new technologies and new medical achievements, hitherto not contemplated. How will they approach them? God's word is eternal and never changes. It will be important for future generations to adhere to that word in order to remain on high moral ground. To do otherwise will expand the moral crisis existing today until the dignity and sanctity of life no longer exist.

Glossary

Blastocyte – a hollow ball of cells filled with fluid that forms four days after fertilization.

Chimera – an organism formed from cells of at least two different genotypes.

Clone – the replication of somatic cells by asexual means.

Diploid – two sets of chromosomes, twice the haploid with 46 (in humans).

Embryo – technically refers to the stage of development from the 3rd week to the 8th week.

Fetus – stage of human development from 9th week until birth.

Genome – the complete set of genetic material of an organism.

Haploid – one set of chromosomes in a gamete (23 in humans).

Genotype – genetic constitution of an individual.

Karyotyping – the testing for chromosome abnormalities.

Mieoses – process of division of a diploid cell resulting in two nuclei with half the number of present chromosomes.

Mitosis – process of the doubling of chromosomes then separation starting with diploid cell and ending with two diploid cells.

Morula – after fertilization and proliferation at the 12 to 16 stage (3 days) – appearance of a mulberry.

Mosaic – varying genetic expression in an individual composed of two genetically different types.

Glossary

Phenotype – the observable characteristics of an individual.

Pre- or Pro-embryo - development stage from the first division (cleavage) until the beginning of the primitive streak (3 weeks).

Pre-implantation Genetic Diagnosis – genetic testing done on fertilized eggs to detect congenital disease.

Primitive streak – the lining up of cells in development on the caudal end of the embryonic disc thus demonstrating the earliest evidence of embryonic axis and the embryo proper.

Totipotent – the capacity of a cell to produce a whole total/embryo or fetus with all its embryonic membranes and tissue.

Stem Cell – totipotent cells found in the early embryo also found in umbilical chord blood.

Zygote – the fertilized egg before cellular division or cleavage has occurred.

Doctors Ron, Bo, and John Kirkwood are brothers in the flesh as well as brothers in Christ and practice Family Medicine in Pasadena, Texas.

www.ingramcontent.com/pod-product-compliance
Lightning Source LLC
Chambersburg PA
CBHW061956070426
42450CB00011BA/3122